Yes, There Will Be Singing

POETS ON POETRY

Marilyn Hacker and Kazim Ali, Series Editors
Donald Hall, Founding Editor

New titles

Kazim Ali, *Orange Alert*
David Baker, *Show Me Your Environment*
Martín Espada, *The Lover of a Subversive Is Also a Subversive*
Marilyn Hacker, *Unauthorized Voices*
Andrew Hudgins, *Diary of a Poem*
T. R. Hummer, *Available Surfaces*
Lawrence Joseph, *The Game Changed*
Marilyn Krysl, *Yes, There Will Be Singing*
David Mason, *Two Minds of a Western Poet*
Cole Swensen, *Noise That Stays Noise*

Recently published

Meena Alexander, *Poetics of Dislocation*
Annie Finch, *The Body of Poetry*
Sandra M. Gilbert, *On Burning Ground*
Grace Schulman, *First Loves and Other Adventures*
Reginald Shepherd, *Orpheus in the Bronx*
Reginald Shepherd, *A Martian Muse*

Also available, collections by

Elizabeth Alexander, A. R. Ammons, John Ashbery, Robert Bly, Philip Booth, Marianne Boruch, Hayden Carruth, Amy Clampitt, Alfred Corn, Douglas Crase, Robert Creeley, Donald Davie, Thomas M. Disch, Ed Dorn, Tess Gallagher, Dana Gioia, Linda Gregerson, Allen Grossman, Thom Gunn, Rachel Hadas, John Haines, Donald Hall, Joy Harjo, Robert Hayden, Edward Hirsch, Daniel Hoffman, Jonathan Holden, John Hollander, Paul Hoover, Andrew Hudgins, Laura (Riding) Jackson, Josephine Jacobsen, Mark Jarman, Galway Kinnell, Kenneth Koch, John Koethe, Yusef Komunyakaa, Maxine Kumin, Martin Lammon (editor), Philip Larkin, David Lehman, Philip Levine, Larry Levis, John Logan, William Logan, William Matthews, William Meredith, Jane Miller, David Mura, Carol Muske, Alice Notley, Geoffrey O'Brien, Gregory Orr, Alicia Suskin Ostriker, Ron Padgett, Marge Piercy, Anne Sexton, Karl Shapiro, Charles Simic, William Stafford, Anne Stevenson, May Swenson, James Tate, Richard Tillinghast, C. K. Williams, Alan Williamson, Charles Wright, James Wright, John Yau, and Stephen Yenser

Marilyn Krysl

Yes, There Will Be Singing

THE UNIVERSITY OF MICHIGAN PRESS

Ann Arbor

Published in the United States of America by
The University of Michigan Press
Manufactured in the United States of America
♾ Printed on acid-free paper

2017 2016 2015 2014 4 3 2 1

A CIP catalog record for this book is available from the British Library.
ISBN 978-0-472-03602-8 (pbk. : alk. paper)
ISBN 978-0-472-12056-7 (e-book)

For Riva and Rohan
and the hundreds of students
who over years of trial and error
taught me how to teach

Acknowledgments

Grateful acknowledgment is given to the editors of the publications listed below in which these essays first appeared. Most of these essays have been revised for this publication. Most quotations in this book fall under fair use provisions, but where extended excerpts and whole poems have been quoted, permission has been sought.

American Poetry Review: "Sacred and Profane: The Sestina as Rite"; "Sad Sestina" is from *The Horse Fair: Poems*, by Robin Becker, © 2000. Reprinted by permission of Pittsburgh University Press. *American Poetry Review* also published "Collaboration: Theme and Variations," which appears here as "The Healing Arts: Collaboration."

Bloomsbury Review: "Not 'I.'"

Contemporary Poetry Review: "Teaching Taste, Making Soul."

Field: "The Leper's Rattle": Tribute to Anna Akhmatova.

Gently Read Literature: "Ardor and the Sestina"; James Cummins' "Tiresias," from *Still Some Cake*, © 2012 by James Cummins. Carnegie Mellon University Press.

"Looking to See How the Eyes Inhabit Dark, Wondering about Light," from *Shoulda Been Jimi Savannah*. © 2012 by Patricia Smith. Coffee House Press.

"Ingrid Wendt: Nonviolent Woman Warrior" first appeared as the essay "The Poetry of Nonviolence: Marilyn Krysl on Ingrid Wendt."

High Plains Literary Review: "Dirt."

Iowa Review: "Marianne Moore's Prose: Antithesis as Modus Operandi."

Journal of Higher Education: "Under the Jade Vault Lei Feng Salutes Mark Twain" appears here in an extended, revised version entitled *Romola: Renegade in the People's Republic of China.*

Many Mountains Moving: "W. S. Merwin's 'One Story': A Tribute."

North American Review: "Temple Beggar: Madurai."

Notre Dame Review: "Water Rites."

One Word—Contemporary Writers on the Words They Love or Loathe, Sarabande Books, 2010, Molly McQuade, Editor: "Filthy."

Prairie Schooner: "Two Motion Fast Happening God."

Redactions: Spiritual Pilgrimage: On Karen Swenson's *A Pilgrim into Silence,* Mary Crow's *I Have Tasted the Apple.*

Witness: "Beautiful Trouble."

Women's Review of Books: Margo Berdeshevsky's "A Passage in Wilderness"; "The Poet in Wartime: Marilyn Hacker's 'Names'"; Venus Khoury-Ghata's "Nettles."

Contents

VI. Poetry and the Healing Arts

Preface

Back in the late 1800s the renowned dancer Isadora Duncan changed dance forever by dancing on the London stage barefoot—after which all Europe was at her feet. She made a remark that still reverberates. *All art is religious,* she said, *or else it is mere merchandise.*

The word *merchandise* calls up our outer, public lives of work, consumption, pressure, speed. But the word *religious* evokes the inner life of emotion, contemplation, dreaming, creating. Imagine walking past New York City's plate-glass windows where mannequins display the latest fashions, and in the middle of the block coming upon a cathedral. Imagine climbing the steps, going inside, putting the drug called acquisition on hold and opening yourself to feeling, to the religious life of art, the life of the heart.

It is good that we have at our disposal both worlds. We need the noisy street where, in brief connection, we brush against each other, and we also need solitude and its spirited quiet. But we need these two locations at different times. When I write I enter a space/time bubble where I don't have to hurry. The bustle of buying and selling will go on indefinitely, but in my sanctuary this rushing, gobbling world can't touch me. I enter my cloister without a plan. Now and again an essay or a poem of a story appears on the page. Then another, and another. Now do with these motley essays what you will.

I.

Origins

Not "I"

> If you are on earth, you are on a landscape, and you can get off it for a little, like Michael Jordan, but not for too long.
>
> —Ed Dorn

I try to imagine that first English-speaking *Homo sapiens* who imitated a Magpie's feisty insistence and coined the pronoun "I." I, I, I, we squawk, I'm a poet! But no poet writes alone. We are never not part of the live warp and weft of earth's breathing, changing interdependencies. As a child I spent rich swaths of time at my Kansas grandparents' wheat and cattle farm where I experienced this interdependence as play. I mimicked birds' twitter and song, and I put my ear to the ground's hum and hummed along.

I sang poems to chickens, conversed with sunflowers. I believed that the words people uttered came from deep, oracular orifices in the earth. Words rose to earth's surface, currents of air blew these sounds into my mouth. I was supported by swallows flying overhead and by earth and its underground rivers of speech. When I learned to spell, poems appeared on my tablet. My grandmother said I'd made them up. I said no—the words flew up from the grass and into me.

I resembled the Greeks' Aeolian harp which stood on the earth where the wind might sweep through and play melodies. I sensed the scientific fact that my body is inextricably enmeshed with the natural world outside my body and with the one hundred trillion microbiota "inside" my body. If my grandmother were alive, I'd point out that every person who refers to themselves as "I" is connected to and dependent on this encompassing mesh. Think of King's *Letter from the Birmingham Jail.* "We are caught in an inescapable network of mutuality, tied in a single garment of destiny."

For the sake of convenience, the independent pronoun "I" has become a hallowed and misleading convention. The pronoun "I" makes poets sound as though we're not fleeting events, not live linkages in a linguistic progression through time, but stolid solids. I beg to disagree. Humility Training has taught me that I'm made up of a lifetime of momentary events, events sometimes graced by a wave of words.

Notice that Flannery O'Connor avoids the pronoun "I" and says instead that "in art the self becomes self-forgetful in order to meet the demands of the thing . . . being made."[1] She depicts herself as a humble receiver, a *location* where utterance emerges.

The playwright Harold Pinter said of his play *The Birthday Party:*

> The thing germinated and bred itself. It proceeded according to its own logic. . . . The writing arranged itself with no trouble into dramatic terms. . . . The play was now its own world. . . . determined by its own engendering image.[2]

Germinated. Bred. Like flora and fauna, "the writing arranged itself with no trouble."

Like most writers I spoke for many years as though I'd invented "my" poems, but this was a lie of convenience. Now, when words appear on the page, I understand that I'm a live "place" where language declares itself through me. Instead of saying that I write poems, I've begun to say that I'm lucky to be a place where poems sometime appear.

But, you object, this assertion that language comes from our live surround ignores a poet's "labor." Yes there's labor in "receiving," and that labor is the willingness to wait and to welcome the mesh of the offering world. Revising a draft of a poem may seem an act performed by the poet—excising, adding, rearranging the furniture. But even revising isn't solely the poet's work because the poet is embedded in the poem's network and in earth's live networks. Annie Dillard described the linkage of the poet to the supporting world as "unmerited grace."

> You break your heart, your back, your brain, and then . . . from the corner of your eye you see motion. Something is moving through the air and headed your way. . . . it has two white wings. It flies directly at you. . . .[3]

Richard Rodriguez also speaks of words as autonomous beings.

> I write things, but I don't write them. They write themselves. All the metaphors that writers use imply that the writer is more passive than active agent in all this: Holy Ghost, the muse, the graces. . . . you are forced to just wait there like an idiot. . . .[4]

"We don't obtain the most precious gifts," Simone Weil wrote, "by going in search of them, but by waiting for them. There is a way of waiting . . . for the right word to come of itself at the end of our pen, while we merely reject all inadequate words."[5]

So who is this scribe who sits and waits? The "poet," but not the poet alone. The poet-in-the-mesh-of-the-world. When words come into us, we are taking the wafer in our mouths, we are swallowing the wine. The world around us resonates, and we become larger and kinder. We remember then, gratefully, that when we listen the land will speak. I want to speak with D. H. Lawrence's accuracy. *Not I,* he said, *but the wind that blows through me.*

We who stand before audiences at poetry festivals have the opportunity to point out that readers too are a crucial part of writing's living, breathing network. Lewis Hyde has said that if a work of art is to live, it must keep moving. When a reader consumes a poem, what she passes on into the surrounding world is her changed perspective and transformed actions. In this way readers are poets' collaborators. But most readers aren't conscious of their collaboration. They imagine the poet an autonomous genius. How do you write these poems, a reader asks, out of thin air? "Thin air" indeed—for air delivers each breath without which no word can be spoken.

I imagine a reader, opened and energized by the words in a

poem, leaving the book open to that last page, and going out into late morning air. That pine tree across the gulley has been there seventy years, but now it seems washed clean of the grime of the ordinary. The grasses whisper *come here, come here,* and the reader feels energized and remembers a prior intention to bike instead of driving, so as to put less soot into the air.

I think of this reader and of the words I heard rising from my grandmother's pastures. When a reader asks what time of day and what location I find most conducive to writing poems, she has offered me opportunity to respond, not with a casual "I do it at a desk from nine to one," but in sensuous, revelatory detail. Writers, I tell her, are scribes taking dictation from the earthy network, and reader-receivers are crucial links through which the work of art keeps moving, and keeps improving the world it moves through.

The poet Alicia Ostriker said, "I am an aperture through which the words arrive." Arrive from where? The poet Ruth Stone reported that at certain times she could "feel a poem coming over the landscape," and declared that the poem's words arrived on a "thunderous train of air."[6] And from where? From earth's interdependent networks that have evolved for billions of years.

"I've crawled from the mire," Theodore Roethke wrote, "privy to oily fungus and the algae of standing waters, / honored . . . by the ancient fellowship of rotten stems."[7]

Notes

1. Lewis Hyde, *The Gift: Imagination and the Erotic Life of Property* (New York: Random House, 1983), p. 150.

2. Ibid., p. 145.

3. Annie Dillard, *The Writing Life* (New York: Harper and Row, 1989), p. 75.

4. Jo Scott-Coe, Richard Rodriguez interview, *Narrative Magazine.com.*

5. Simone Weil, *Waiting for God* (New York: Harper and Row, 1973), p. 113.

6. Elisabeth Gilbert, quoting Ruth Stone on YouTube.

7. Theodore Roethke in Lewis Hyde, *The Gift: Imagination and the Erotic Life of Property* (New York: Random House, 1983), p. 156.

Dirt's Minion

> Worship means not to figure out, not to analyze, not to pin down, but deeply to value.
> —William Bryant Logan

I was born in the middle of the Twentieth Century on the Great Plains, place of stillness and tornado, heat and blizzard. Earth's two human truths, beauty and wrath, were just other versions of the weather. And part of that weather was the language of the King James Bible my grandparents read aloud from every morning. I was two, three and four, listening, rapt, to this language rolling from their mouths. *Many waters cannot quench love, neither can the floods drown it.* At first I heard only the sound of that language. I listened to its musical cadences, and was rocked by those cadences. Only much later did I begin to understand that these were the words of God, and that he wanted us to take heed and distinguish right from wrong.

The Bible's language reminded me of my stately grandmother and her land, where corn, wheat and sorghum flourished on acres of dependable dirt. She was a benevolent force moving through the world, and like the men who worked for my grandfather through the harvest, I was smitten. I needed to hear her voice, watch her walk.

"Get your hat," she would say, putting on her wide-brimmed straw.

It pained me that I never succeeded in liking the feel of a hat, but I put it on, took her hand, and we stepped out into the live, vibrating world. Humans and birds, air and water, stones and soil—we were all alive, and we all recognized each other. And since I was the youngest, the one nearest to the ground, I noticed something special beneath my feet: an element called dirt.

Dirt was the earth's floor, everywhere, and right here. It was the most basic of materials, elemental and magical. I knew places where dirt was dried and hard, other places where it was soft and powdery—ground's talcum. When I helped my grandmother weed the garden, fat worms drilled their passageways through topsoil, giving the roots of plants an airing, and I scooped up a handful. Dirt, I imagined, was like me: it liked being handled. I crumbled it with my fingers, helping it breathe.

Later I would learn that ancient peoples believed that gems, stones and metals lived a life like animals lived. Thales, a Greek, believed chunks of amber were alive. Had I known this, I'd have declared myself the Thales of dirt. Scientists hadn't yet discovered the microorganisms which prosper in dirt, but I sensed that dirt was beneficial. I talked to dirt and patted it, told it stories, sang to it. And I assured dirt that it wasn't dirty. It was a sacred powder that had the power to make plants, animals and people grow.

The earth was made from dirt, and the earth, according to the Bible, was holy ground. My grandmother let me get high on the glory of being dirty, and I got as dirty as I could, and stayed dirty for as long as I liked. One day I piled dirt in the cracked bluewillow bowl my grandmother had given me, and set it on top of a box: this was my altar. In the middle of the bowl I placed a single candle and lit it.

"Let there be light!" I shouted. "And darkness, and the waters! And fish and robins! And the snake! And pancakes and syrup! Let there be lots of stars every night," I demanded. "And give us all the dirt you've got."

Stunned by heat those long afternoons, I stirred water into a pan of dirt. So unlike each other, dirt and water, but together they became a third thing: the thick, primal goop of creation. A long swath of afternoon lay before me, and I mixed a pan of mud, and from this rich, wet muck I sculpted Adam and Eve. I gave them arms, legs, faces. Eve had breasts, Adam a penis. In the beginning, the Bible said, they couldn't see each other's nakedness. But I thought blindness was unfair, so I gave them eyes.

Presto: they saw me, and their mouths cried out for sustenance. So I mixed a pan of mud brownies and baked them on the hot metal slab of my grandfather's combine. When the brownies were done, I fed my creations. While they ate, I recited verses from the Bible. *From dust thou comest,* I intoned. Everyone and every thing came from dirt, and it was obvious that we all should be friendly. *Do unto others as you would have them do unto you.*

In a solitary moment, I knelt, laid my ear against the ground, and heard, far down, a subtle grumbling, like distant thunder. It was the moan of a creature, the audible irritation of a great being. A thing as big as the earth, I thought, had its own plan. It was fine that humans dug up topsoil to plant crops, but beyond that, I believed, we should refrain from meddling. If earth wanted to move the furniture around, it could make an earthquake. Who were we to interfere?

I wanted whatever changed to do the changing itself. Gardening was fair, because we massaged dirt and let it breathe, and we fed it compost. But please, no men with shovels and picks, hacking a mountainside, hungry for gold. I was against building dams or drilling oil wells, and I disapproved of bulldozers leaving the imprint of tire treads.

"Why are those men doing that?" I asked my grandmother.

"They're building us a road," she said.

"But we already have one!"

How many roads did it take to get from one place to another? One, I thought, was plenty.

Days later, one of Adam's arms broke off. Eve's feet began to crumble. I repaired my creations, and this worked for a time. But things made from dirt were subject to disintegration, and a day came when I could no longer postpone the funeral. I scooped out a grave and laid my dried mud mummies in. *From dust thou cometh and to dust thou shalt return.* The things of this world appeared, stayed a while, then disintegrated. I stood over my creations with the hose, helping Eve and Adam fall back into the earth they'd come from.

Decades have passed since I served as dirt's minion, and still we know only enough to realize that human ignorance is vast and dangerous. And we find ourselves in a curious position. We're sentient beings, a living part of the data, and at the same time we're observers of that data. We can trace much of our human responsibility for how life on earth evolves, and when we reckon up our part of the damage, we understand that we are not heroic. We mount a campaign here, while ignoring a frightening reckoning just over there beyond that hilltop. We say we're concerned—a word that merely hedges our fleshy responsibility.

For these reasons I would mix again some dirt, some water, and fashion another Eve, another Adam. Both would have legs, arms, hands, a nose, mouth, ears and genitals. And this time too I would give them eyes. Look: They gaze at each other, and go on gazing, and when they have looked their fill, they survey their surroundings. Was that a sound, over there where the leaves moved? Eve pokes Adam. He looks where she's pointing. Leaves? A bird? Sunlight, a breeze, insects. Grasses. These supposedly discrete and separate things are one singleness, a weaving of the myriad strands into one felt field.

Now Adam and Eve notice there's something in the air, an animation, an expectancy. The clearing where they sit has a life of its own, a life that will go on without them. Eve picks up a handful of dirt and pours this dirt into Adam's palm. His fingers register dirt's texture, its fineness. There's something here, he thinks, something to notice.

In sunlight dirt looks bright, he says.

Yes, isn't it bright, Eve says. Because it's not a dead thing, but something alive.

They go on sifting dirt through their fingers, and now they feel the life stuff sparking.

It looks like just a handful of dirt, Eve says, but I can feel it breathing.

Adam nods. Yes, he says, and that means that you and I are not alone.

Teaching Taste, Making Soul

Making Soul

Two days after my birth my parents brought me to my grandparents' stone house on the plains. The snow disappeared, wheat sprouted and spread across swaying prairie, and words rose from those fields offering themselves to my grandparents' mouths by way of the King James Bible. *Behold how good and how pleasant it is for brethren to dwell together in unity. It is like the dew that descendeth upon the mountains of Zion.*

My grandparents' voices had the resonance of a cathedral's struck bells. When they read Genesis, it was though Adam and Eve spoke. I listened to incantatory narratives of history, the prophets' scolding authority, the praise and pleading of Psalms, the love poetry of Solomon, the fiery prophecies of Revelation. The King James Bible constituted a fertile sea of language, and I felt no demarcation between myself and these voices, myself and the land. I was an open system, improvising my relation to whinny of stallion and mare, to chicken chatter and Meadowlark call, to my grandmother's voice reciting beneath stars. *Day unto day uttereth speech, and night unto night sheweth knowledge. There is no speech nor language where their voices are not heard.*

That Great Lap the earth was alive, and it offered up words. I heard them rise and passed them on to heifer and rooster, bugs and hogs. "You made up a song!" my grandmother said.

I shook my head. I hadn't made up the song—I'd heard it.

"That song came out of the ground," I said. "I'm singing it on."

My grandmother read me Longfellow's *Song of Hiawatha.* At four I learned to read. There were as many words as bits of limestone gravel on the road so white it looked like a path to heaven. Much later, at ten, on the assumption that the longer a book the more pleasure awaited me, I checked out the longest book in the library: *War and Peace.* On words came, Greek and Roman mythology, *The Secret Garden, Little Women.* In fifth grade I read *Moby Dick* alternating each chapter with a chapter from the adventures of Nancy Drew.

I lived with working-class parents in a house so small and shabby that I trusted only one girlfriend enough to invite her there, and to endure getting through senior year I read all of Faulkner's novels and *The Brothers Karamazov.* Except for a high school lit class where I read Emily Dickinson and Dylan Thomas, education was a series of accidents left largely up to me. Every student of writing needs to read the classics, and by reading at random, I'd inadvertently devised a curriculum for myself.

I remember staring at a word until that word became not ink on a page but live sound vibrating in space, flooding me, billowing me open. To be one of the places where language appeared of its own accord, entered me and then emerged into the world—what more could I possibly want? *My imagination is a monastery,* Keats remarked in my senior English textbook, *and I am its monk.* He had described me.

I began to write poems which I showed to two kind teachers. That spring, when a family friend left a religious magazine at our house, I wrote a story about a man who carries Christ's cross a while so that Christ can take a break, and mailed it to the magazine. The magazine sent me a check for $50. A month later the poems I'd shown my English teachers won me a full tuition scholarship to the first year of University. I was on my way to Shakespeare, Yeats, Auden, H.D., Virginia Woolf, Elizabeth Bishop, and on my way to my own serviceable, edgy, whimsical style. I'd also begun the process of transformation that Keats called *making soul.*

Taste and Making Soul

Taste has no system and no proofs, Susan Sontag remarked. But I submit that taste can be measured by how thoroughly a work of art enlarges the artist's sensibility and soul. Poets know that making soul requires reading classics, for it's by experiencing the expanded minds of literary forebears that we grow into our own concentration and abandon, our raging fire and contemplative stillness. Our lives are then grist for the creative mill.

Do you not see how necessary a world of pains and troubles is, Keats wrote, *to school an intelligence and make it a soul?* Keats invokes "pains and troubles" both as poets' subject matter and as poets' transformative goad. It's those pains and troubles—and joys, ecstasies—that nudge us to step off the cliff blindfolded and see if we can walk on the water down below.

Making Soul as the Standard for Judging Taste

There is the soul of the artist, and there are the souls of those who experience the artist's work. Through childhood and adolescence I'd read without judgment. Reading was an act of merging with the text, becoming one with it. Fortunately my random reading had included that classic cornerstone of Western literature, the King James Bible. I'd read it like every other book with no purpose in mind other than pleasure.

In my Junior year I carried on a love affair with Auden. Because I'd read Yeats' *Easter, 1916,* I recognized its echo in *September 1, 1939.* All that year I walked the campus with the line "we must love one another or die" zinging through me. That poem transformed me, and it was the experience of being transformed that rendered this poem an instance of high art. I would go on to memorize Auden's *In Memory of W. B. Yeats,* and later to admire Walcott's elegy for Auden himself. But it was Auden's elegy for Yeats that had set the bar of taste high. The poem spoke to my brooding about spirituality and politics, and it demonstrated the sheer power certain lyric devices can exert to transform us. It also positioned me to favor both "free verse" lyric and formal lyric equally, and confirmed that free and formal verse can marry within a single poem, and the marriage thrive. Eventually I moved on, but Auden's line has remained with me like the scar from my appendectomy.

The Impact of Taste on Creativity in Both High and Low Art

Rebel angel Salvador Dali was expelled from the Academia, an art school, in 1926, shortly before his finals, when he stated that no one on the faculty was competent to examine him. He held himself in high regard, and remarked: *It is good taste, and good taste alone, that possesses the power to sterilize and is always the first handicap to any creative functioning.*

Some may agree with Dali and with Picasso who said *Ah, good taste! What a dreadful thing! Taste is the enemy of creativeness.* But whether one possesses "good" taste also depends on who is judging and by what standard. Assume for a moment that Sontag's remark that taste has no system and no proofs refers to the general reader. Yes, in a cross section of the reading public, readers' tastes will be as idiosyncratic as choosing from a rack of dresses. A literary historian, on the other hand, will read for comprehensiveness. And one literary critic might read with specific historical precedents in mind, while another who fancies him- or herself an arbiter of taste reads to bolster or to decimate the careers of rising stars.

Questions of taste also call up high and low art. Is doggerel high art or low? Is Part Three of David Rothman's "Three Variations on a Theme by Jim Hall" which delivers the release of laughter high art or low? If a poem strikes deep chords in us—if, as in the case of Rothman's poem, amused release constitutes a species of transcendence—do the labels *low art* and *high art* simply dissolve in our laughter? And if I were to limit my discussion of taste to what I consider high art, would this mark me as a snob?

Making Soul as Proof of Taste Revisited

Those of us who experience a work of art and are transformed by it can attest to that work's transformative power. Take Rilke's *Archaic Torso of Apollo.*

> We cannot know his legendary head
> with eyes like ripening fruit. And yet his torso

is still suffused with brilliance from inside,
like a lamp, in which his gaze, now turned to low,

gleams in all its power. Otherwise
the curved breast could not dazzle you so, nor could
a smile run through the placid hips and thighs
to that dark center where procreation flared.

Otherwise this stone would seem defaced
beneath the translucent cascade of the shoulders
and would not glisten like a wild beast's fur:

would not, from all the borders of itself,
burst like a star: for here there is no place
that does not see you. You must change your life.

Rilke's poem asserts that we *can* discriminate levels of taste by experiencing works of art and noting the degree to which each one gives us a heavenly, transcendent kick in the pants.

The Freedom to Teach Ourselves Taste

I think back to childhood where I read assiduously, choosing at random from a wide array of contrasting works. I was unique, only I could be myself, and what I happened to choose to read would begin to make my soul. Now when I teach, that intuitive history spurs me to insist that students read a good amount of classic poetry. I also suggest particular works which I suspect may be pivotal for a particular student. And I give the student the permission I gave myself to choose intuitively from the widest, idiosyncratic array of tasteful and tasteless reading.

The Right Teacher for a Particular Student

I entered University with scant worldly knowledge. But because I'd won a scholarship, the poet Ralph Salisbury invited me into his senior level poetry workshop. Salisbury, half Scot and half Cherokee, had lived a harrowing life, and he recognized that I was too sheltered and inexperienced to understand how fortunate I was. Later, when I heard the testimonies of both female and male students who had been exploited or ignored, I recognized that Salisbury had respected, honored and nurtured me. He'd saved my inner life, the life that matters, by urging me to write my way through life's inevitable suffering, and to transform that suffering into soul.

It took years for me to grasp the magnitude of his gift. In the meantime, feeling my way forward, I kept reading, teaching myself taste. There was something magical about being me on a particular day at a particular time in a particular library, browsing. I wanted the one book, which, on that day, would speak like babbling water to me alone. I wanted the experience Jane Hirshfield describes in *Nine Gates*. "Free to remain still and wondering amid the mysteries of mind and world, we arrive, for a moment, at a kind of fullness that overspills into everything. One breath taken completely; one poem, fully written, fully read—in such a moment anything can happen."[1]

Note

1. Jane Hirshfield, *Nine Gates: Entering the Mind of Poetry* (New York: HarperCollins, 1997), p. 32.

Filthy

My father mowed the lawn, cleaned the mower, then peeled off his sweaty tee, the grass and oil stained pants. My mother tossed them into the laundry.

"These are filthy," she said. "I'll have to scrub them by hand."

I carried my mother's word *filthy* to the basin in which I made mud pies from water and dirt. Filthy: I felt with my mouth the fricative *F*, the long purl of the *L*, the breathy *H*. The word tasted delicious. Filthy, I crooned over my basin of mud, this goopy, good, nasty malleability.

Mud had texture I liked to feel with my hands. It was made from water and dirt, the world's basic ingredients. From dust thou cometh, the Bible said, and to dust thou shalt return—even people were made from mud. Therefore filthy could not be bad.

> Filth, n. (ME., *filthe, fulthe, felthe*; AS. *Fylthe* base of *ful*). 1. foul dirt; disgusting matter. 2. feces.

Filth: the polite decry it, and the well-off hire help to disappear it. Though even the modern aristocrat wipes his own ass and must notice this congress with his own filth. Let's hope the experience humbles him.

Feces gets right to the bottom of things. We are in the toilet here. But though feces are filthy, feces are also ordinary, necessary, humble and ubiquitous as breath. Bottom basic. Bodies cannot choose not to deliver their daily filth—teeth, hair, the flaking off of thousands of bits of skin—and feces.

But I had seen animals eat feces. Behold, in those moments filth was food—like the mud pies I fed to my mud Adam and Eve instead of an apple. Secretly—I did not tell my mother—I declared the word *filthy* shriven of its negative meaning. I worked the word around in my mouth, whispered it, spoke it. It began to sound more and more ordinary, less and less loaded with negative connotation, more and more neutral. Then I decided to sing it. *Filthy, filthy, filthy! Filthy* became in my mouth an anthem of triumph.

The word *filthy* ascended until it was right up there with *blessed.*

Was this merely joyful semantic play in which I defied the powerful literal? Or was perceiving the word *filthy* as a kind of beauty a way of defying my mother's insistence on protecting me from the world I longed to explore? When I needed to use a public toilet, my mother insisted on placing the paper shield on the seat.

"These seats are filthy. We don't know who sat here." There were people who seldom bathed, she told me, and they sat on public toilets without a thought for the welfare of others.

Who were these people?

"Vagrants. They don't work, so they don't have a place to live or a bathtub."

After defining the word *filth, Webster's* proceeds: see *foul. Foul,* from Middle English and Anglo-Saxon, also akin to German's *faul,* meaning rotten, putrid, lazy. Lazy? Here was the link between *filthy* and my mother's uneasiness about "vagrants." The word *filthy* lies cheek by jowl with lazy, and thus not to bathe might well lead, in my mother's mind, to poverty.

The poor were different from us: they had way less money.

Then I was ten, and a case of the mumps left me permanently deaf in my left ear. My mother, intending sympathy, said "You poor thing."

Poor me, I imagined, as in ragged clothes, no money, starving and dirty. Suddenly I became curious about the poor. How, I wondered, had they become poor? Everyone gave the same answer: they'd failed to practice frugality.

Distinctions blazed: the poor might get drunk, but we stayed sober. They might have "diseases." We did not. But beneath these distinctions lay the unspoken assumption that Americans were self-reliant people who went into business and prospered. Those who did not prosper had not worked hard enough. They were lazy—and thus shamefully Un-American. The tautology was crazy-making: the poor were shameful because it was shameful to be poor.

Now I understand that when my mother used the word *filthy*, she invoked her worst fear: if we did not work hard AND keep ourselves spanking clean, we would become destitute—without even a toilet of our own.

But what about money, as in *filthy lucre*? We want as much money as we can get our hands on. Become *filthy rich*, and you spring into the upper class where the expression *filthy rich* carries no shameful association. On the contrary it identifies the rich as privileged. Nor does the laziness of the rich carry a foul odor. Their laziness is a badge of wealth like their Ferraris.

We envy the lazy wealthy who are lazy because they can afford to be.

A bath, and I'm reborn. I enjoy feeling clean. Then slowly my body wears through time, and in the garden, weary and elated with the pleasure of digging and lifting shovelfuls of soil, every pore feels opened and emptied out with effort. Sweat and dirt on my skin seem an earned badge of blessing. I've come through the ceremony of hard labor, and now the word *filthy* rises up, but—how can this be?—it means its opposite.

I'm fully filthy in the best possible way.

The word *filthy* has become celebratory.

A friend in a hurry tracks mud across my kitchen floor. I get down on my knees and scrub. As I scrub, the word *filthy* meshes with my scrubbing, and now, slowly, the word *filthy* fills with an overflowing sensuality. I'm one with my labor, and as I pay close attention, I notice that every cell of me is present, throbbing. I go on scrubbing and now I'm humming the word *filthy*. Singing, I transform the hymn: filthy, filthy, filthy, Lord God Almighty.

Time goes on, and slowly the word *filthy*—and also the floor—become clean. I stand up, feeling as I do after a bath, when I towel off and rise a little into the air.

The floor is clean, and I feel wonderfully filthy. I stand there feeling filthy rich with this word's capital. My investment, linguistically speaking, keeps multiplying. And I would share this word's largesse. As Buddhists say when they repeat the loving kindness phrases, may I be filthy, may you be filthy. May all living beings be filthy.

Filthy slides in and out of its literal meaning as though definition is clothing, and my lover undresses me, kisses my belly and banters.

"Oh you are so filthy!" he says, meaning that I please him greatly.

Today as I ride a bus in the direction of the Homeless Shelter, my mother's voice sits on my shoulder. A man gets on. His jeans are stiff with grime. His shirt's stained, torn, and he smells sweaty. *Foul,* says my mother's voice. *Filthy.*

He doesn't have the fare, so another rider gives it to him. He sits beside me. You might say I'm privileged—I can afford a bus pass, he can't—but on the human level this fact neither exalts me nor damns him. The body is a great equalizer—everybody's got one—and here we are, he and I, wearing our genealogical attire. Our skin is outerwear, and on his forehead a smudge. Dirt under his fingernails. Maybe he worked construction today, or landscaping. Maybe he tried but couldn't find work. Maybe he didn't try. I don't know if he feels himself a failure at this moment or if he's proud of how he's negotiating the day. Sitting beside me he's another weary human like I am, filthy like I am—that word filled to the brim with the body's beauty. We sit in silence, our bodies quietly singing their song of filth: a hymn.

Filthy won't lie still. It rises up and insists on being worthy. It demands equal opportunity with beauty. St. Paul doesn't approve, but filthy doesn't care. It's going to dance naked whenever it wants. It wants to move, to morph, to be here and then gone, a shimmer of light across silk—and at the same time it wants to be resoundingly foul. Filthy wants it both ways—it defies the binary bind. Like the yin/yang nestled into each other's curves, filthy insists on embodying transcendence.

Imagine a crowd of us filling the streets of the metropolis, bodies pouring from side streets onto the central avenue, a great crowd becoming more crowded, more humans attired in the body's frail envelope of flaking skin, all of these bodies in unison intoning the word *filthy,* mouthing it with lips' and tongues' joy, all of us high on a single word's transformation, shouting the word *filthy,* that good, dirty anthem of the human.

Water Rites

In a circle of elms near the stone farmhouse, my grandfather had cemented a shallow pool. I entered this cylinder of shade, lay on my belly. I was four. Fish slid in lazy loops. Domed light arched over this sphere. Only the fish moved, in that other world, the one under water.

I'd heard my grandparents talking about how badly we needed rain. Their faces registered concern. I would have to do something to help, but what? I picked up a twig, dropped it in. The twig floated at the center of concentric ripples. Then, on the opposite rim, something thick and dark slid down to the water and in.

Over it the water closed.

I had seen four legs, a tail.

A breeze stirred the elm leaves. Beyond the rim of shade where there had been sun the grass darkened. Now a god shook the thunder rattle. I had the distinct sense that my toss of that twig had set something large and above us in motion. I leapt up and ran toward the house. My grandmother was kneading dough. Her presence amidst the scent of yeast was reassuring. Bright bursts of speech flared from me, and she nodded. The creature, she told me, was a water dog.

They were shy, she said. I felt a swell of friendliness: so was I. Water dogs resembled lizards, but lizards preferred heat, and drought. Water dogs were heralds of storm. They wove themselves in and out amidst the slippery fish. Then, with a magic flick of their bodies, they wafted this watery atmosphere up to heaven so that it might come down to us as rain. As she spoke, we heard the tick of the first drops.

Centuries before this, my ancestors crowded around the priest at Mt. Lykaios. He prayed, and they watched the slender branch of an oak tree in his hand. When his prayer ended, he offered the branch to the pool. It floated, then began to sink. Something resembling mist rose above the water. Those of my ancestors who were there said the air turned electric. A jagged streak of light cracked across the sky. Afterward an intensity persisted where the streak had been, as though that heat had left its imprint on air. Then all present felt the shudder of thunder. A few minutes later downpour began.

Summoning water is an ancient rite. The priest and I had invoked the serpent goddess. In the Vedas she is Kadru, to the Babylonians Kadi, goddess whose body is a snake with breasts and the shoulders and head of a woman. This serpent embodied a watery form of the energy Hindus call *sakti*: She of the waters above and below the world, waters whose energy moves in a serpentine pattern. Myth tells us she separated a length of this energy from herself, and fashioned it into a wavy slither. She'd made a slickness, but with substance. And with this slipperiness she pleasured herself.

Her offspring are nagis, serpent genies, as sinuous as the water itself. The Greeks thought the nagi ugly: coarse bodied, reptilian, scaled. But the nagi's ugliness confers magical properties. Like water rippling, the nagi's skin slides off, floats away, dissolves. The nagi, bringer of rain, embodies our longing to be reborn.

I have come to Tobacco Caye to pay my respects to Ancestor Water. Lying beside the coral reef off the coast of Belize, this Caye is so small you walk across it in five minutes. The shore is strewn with feathers from cruising Frigate birds, palm branches last night's storm blew down. Where the shore slopes down, a ridge of rain-beaten sand. Stones beside the pier gleam. The water itself seems scrubbed clean.

I walk into this immensity of water. Entering the sea feels like entering another body. "Women's sexual organs," the Diola sing, "are full of water." In Sumerian the letter *a* meant both water and sperm. Some Sakti from that first sea is still in me, and in you, regardless of our gender. I dive down. *Holocentrus ascensionis'* ribbony fins resemble pastel chiffon. Groupers are slices of sunlight submerged. Below the coral grass beds nurse fish, and where fish graze and defecate the coral grows faster. I weave amidst the feasting and feel at home. I too have come to feed and be fed by this feeding world.

Afterward, I lie in the shade. *Body of water,* we say. "Let us not impose doctrines upon the landscape," Natalia Rachel Singer writes, or "metaphors of the body." I too would not attribute to nature merely human capacities. But if we can't use the word *body,* how then speak of our long love affair with water?

"Nowadays we prefer to speak of the environment," writes Deborah Tall, "but it too, in its original meaning, is what surrounds us, rather than what we are inextricably involved in." So call it inextricable involvement then. In *The Spell of the Sensuous,* David Abram describes this involvement as a kind of "reciprocal encounter." Living systems continuously perceive and interact with surrounding systems, making finely tuned adjustments. With every sense perception the jig changes, partners grooving with each other even as they reshape the groove. We and the world hail each other, and like the shrug of a jacketed shoulder, shift our chemical balance and proceed.

Just as I feel water against my skin, water registers the space I take up. I float, and water holds my weight. I drink, and water tastes me. Merleau-Ponty called this web of reciprocal encounter the world's *flesh.* Streams, springs, waterfalls and seas of this flesh pulse forth their fluid energy. "They *are,*" Mircea Eliade writes, "and they are *alive.*" Why not say body of water? And why not call ocean our ancestor?

Fluid and androgynous, this forebear gave birth, and fashioned the appropriate elders. "When they went ashore," Rachel Carson writes, "the animals that took up a land life carried with them a part of the sea in their bodies." The signature of that original parent is still in us. Human body hair is not arranged in the pattern of other apes but in the pattern in which water's mantle flows over our bodies as we move through it. Our bodies are three-quarters water, the proportion of water to land on the planet. And sodium, potassium and calcium combine in our blood in almost the same proportion as in the oceans. We're mostly water, with a pinch of salt in our cellular pockets, sloshing from one liquid decision to another.

I was three when my mother took me to the Pacific. The water, rocking, refracting light, reminded me of certain green glass bottles. This was color ceaselessly moving—and sounding. Ocean's voice was guttural, Orphic. When I closed my eyes, its moaning rippled through me. Sound waves replicate the ocean's wave form. The rhythms of our speech echo the liturgy of pouring water. We say of a brook that it babbles, and why not: language, after all, is another bodily gesture rising out of what we are inextricably involved in.

I stood before this ancient, uttering elder. Egyptians imaged masculine and feminine combined in the Nile's floodwaters as the anthropomorphic goddess Hapi. Babylonians projected Apsu and Tiamat, waters whose currents mingled in a single mass. Homer described Oceanus, a river in amorphous space where there was neither sky nor earth. Tethys was figured as the female, but her spiraling mass could not be distinguished from the course of Oceanus itself.

Before me is one body, resounding: Grandfather Ocean, Grandmother Water. I understood this forebear was alive, and very old. Ocean endures, and sea's ceaseless moving seems to neutralize time. Confronted with such persistent immensity, we can imagine nothing before it. "Water," Eliade wrote, "precedes all forms and upholds all creation." *Neither Non-Being nor Being existed then,* intones the Rgveda. *Neither air nor the firmament above existed. What then was moving with such force? Was it the deep and fathomless water?*

Soulful, ruminating, the great body presented itself, and took me in. I felt watched and heard in every cell. I would learn that Sardinians worshiped certain springs and held ordeals there to test a person's truthfulness. The Vedas assert that water seeks the truth, that waves of the ocean keep away lies. I knew instinctively that I dared not dissemble in ocean's presence.

And if water spoke to me, then I might speak to it. I stood on the beach and answered this ancestor with the same *ur* syllables I heard rising out of her. I hissed and groaned. I was murmur and lament and roaring power.

When we returned to the Midwest, I continued this conversation with water. One day I stood on the couch, looking down behind it, listening to my mother and grandmother talk. I announced that there was a stream running behind the couch.

"Don't tell lies," my mother said.

"And what does this water say?" my grandmother asked.

"It's saying you should believe me!"

A generation later this sense of water's knowing came to my four-year-old daughter. One afternoon she squatted at the lake's edge, listening intently. Suddenly she swung around. "If you tell a lie," she said, "the water will hear you."

John Muir lay down on Sierra Nevada granite in order to "think like a glacier." But to think is not the same as to know. Scientists investigating water's knowing have found it sensitive to very slight changes in electrical and magnetic fields. In the thirties Giorgio Piccardi found that the rate of chemical reactions taking place in water solutions was affected by lunar and sunspot cycles, solar eruptions and sudden showers of cosmic rays. Later Theodor Schwenk established that after an eclipse water recorded this dwindling of the light. C. W. Smith of Salford University in Britain concluded that the smallest amounts of allergens diluted out of existence in water had transferred their properties to the dilution, but not chemically. The water in his samples had recorded the allergen's electrical impression and passed it on.

At five I gave not a fig for such figuring. I was already inextricably involved with water. I understood that by its swaying inevitability the water in my basin would tell me how things were. After I'd interrogated the basin, I gathered milkweed and buttercup. Singing, I stirred the blossoms in. The aroma of the petals floated up. With this flowery attention I had made water happy. My grandmother had given me a scrap of leather, and by stretching it over a tin can, I'd made a drum. As the final act in my ceremony I sat cross-legged before the basin, beating out a liquid rhythm, singing.

I didn't know that primitive cultivators believed the beating of a shaman's drum affects the structure of water. Each evening during growing season, these first planters beat a drum beside their buckets. They stirred a bit of soil in clockwise and sang ascending notes. They stirred counterclockwise and sang a descending scale. I hadn't been told these things, and still, at dusk when I went with my grandmother to drive the cows home, I took a jar of my magic water along, sprinkled it at the head of each row of my grandfather's corn.

Engagement with water is a sensuous affair, and we who are smitten are busy with this voluptuous doing. We recognize the erotic when we encounter it, and seek those sites where water issues from the earth: streams, springs, wells, the fountains in sunstruck plazas. Even a sprinkler's whir is ardent undercurrent. The garden hose gushes, and I drink. Drink, and offer myself to be drunk. No showers for me. I prefer immersion.

Immersion is the body at play—pleasure for pleasure's sake, mine and water's—the two of us tasting the slippery texture of our skins. To be, in my strong body, and to enter water, to push against it as it gives, to stroke myself through its slickness—this is my preferred consummation. "We could imagine disease not just as a physical phenomenon," writes Thomas Moore, "but as the failure of the body to find its pleasure." Swimming, I become like those ailing children dipped three times into the well of Saint Mandron, in Cornwall. Water, like a mother's kiss, makes things better.

Shoreline is a boundary. When I slide in buoyed by my element, I leave behind the body weighted down by gravity. Every time we bathe another border goes. Bits of our skin slough off like the serpent's. A morning bath re-enacts a birth, and in this washing we prepare to enter the diurnal, but as though for the first time. And if at evening we seek the shore, it is because we long to be reborn. "From the point of view of water," Eliade writes, "human life is something fragile that must periodically be engulfed, because it is the fate of all forms to be dissolved in order to reappear."

Ablution echoes the annual dipping of statues of the Great Goddess. Deities, like mortals, must refurbish their vitality, and it was understood that immersion would revamp their good will and generosity. Like us, Aphrodite, Athena, and the Virgin Mary have enjoyed this ritual plunge and been revived.

A breeze rattles the palms' fringe. At dinner there's talk of a storm. I go to my cabin, ready by light of an oil lamp. Sound of breakers flowing up over sand. Lulled by this lustrum, I fall asleep. Later I wake in the dark: downpour batters the tin roof. What twig dropped into what pool has thrown up this storm?

Thomas Merton said that as long as the rain spoke, he would listen. I listen, and remember there are places in the ocean that resemble a war-ravaged nation. The waters record the increase of red tides, Tributyltin in the tissues of invertebrates. They record epidemics among shellfish, the bleaching and the death of corals. They register dumps of plutonium, of chlorine, of the 22.3 million barrels of petroleum spilled each year, and of the release into the deep basins of cadmium, iron, zinc, arsenic. The waters record the presence of lead in the North Sea, of nitrogen in the Mediterranean. And where the Mississippi empties into the Gulf, the waters record that four thousand square kilometer dead zone where there is almost no oxygen. They record the demise of salt marsh and mangrove, mourn the dearth of dolphin, whale, seals. The faces of dead sea cows washed up on the North Carolina coast tell us the oceans too have their disappeared, refugees unable to go home.

Annie Dillard writes that she would like to learn from wild animals "the dignity of living without bias or motive." Water and sand do not pass judgment. Air does not present an affidavit. Fire does not assign blame. Feeling is what the elements offer, and tonight the rain sounds like grieving. I lie back in the storm's duration, but I do not invent homilies to the effect that the sweep of time will heal the waters. Instead I imagine that time when earth's crust cooled enough that the falling rain did not immediately evaporate but began to collect in earth's basins. "These rains fell continuously," Rachel Carson wrote, "day and night, days passing into months, into years, into centuries." *Where wast thou when I laid the foundations of the earth? Who shut up the sea with doors, when it brake forth, as if it had issued out of the womb?* Like Job, I'm humbled by not knowing. I listen while the water around me has its own grieving way.

If wetness speaks of grief, it speaks also of benediction. I remember Carl, in his sixties, in the hospital where I worked as a nurse's aide. Cancer wore at him slowly, increments of change like water lapping a shore. When he died and his family finished their farewells, it fell to me to prepare his body. As I washed him, I became a series of linked motions: the raising of a hand, the bowing of a head, the opening of a palm. The stories say that to get to the other side, the dead must cross water in darkness. The water I washed Carl with was the water of that crossing, lapping the sides of the boat.

Once when I worked in a country torn by war, there came moments when the palpable despair in those around me seemed scarcely bearable. In scorching heat I went to the sea at midday, left a towel on the sand, entered the water. I swam steadily and hard, deliberate with need. I wanted to be abraded, polished like a rock turned in ocean's crucible. When I walked up the slope onto shore, my towel lay before me, a flare. I sank down and let myself drift there in the caul of exhaustion.

When I woke, the sun was low. The shore seemed scattered with yellow blossoms. Then I saw one cluster of petals skitter. As far down the strand as I could see in either direction, hundreds of tiny crabs, the bright yellow of the crayon box, had come out of hiding. They seemed bright bits of a generous wetness, an offering tossed up from the depths onto an altar. I had lain down in sanctuary. I'd awakened at the center of ten thousand prayers.

On those occasions when we feel cast out of the human world, when we want to step back from civilization and feel just how animal we really are, the natural world rises up as refuge. It is our horizon note, Eliade's foundation, the bottom line. The Ancient One, life giving death bringer, is always there. She conducts ablutions ceaselessly, and, if we join her, takes us in.

For make no mistake: our desecration of the cathedral does not mark the end of our longing for union. No nation or religion has ever put a stop to water worship, though Christians in the Middle Ages tried, beginning with the Second Council of Arles in 443, continuing until the Council of Treves in 1227. Finally the church gave up. I imagine the Pope bearing the record of the Council's proceedings to the river, tearing parchment to bits, letting these scraps fall onto the water.

For we who are grateful for water like to give it a little something. Each time I visit a watery source, I leave a feather, a nut, a few petals, a handful of meal. When the Masai approach a river, they tear off a handful of grass and toss it in. We are doing what pilgrims at the lake of Saint Andeol in the Aubrac mountains did when they gave the water bits of linen, a piece of cake, a shirt or a coat. What the Trojans did when they sacrificed live horses to the raging river. What Greek priests did when they slaughtered oxen for the god of the sea.

Language is bodily gesture, and gesture is language. I enter the waters here one last time. Below me, the coral polyps seem a visual chorus, each uttering its note. I slither through this surge of oratorio, then roll onto my back, let sky see the length of me. I'm aware of the salt in this water, adding density to water's texture, and the taste, on my lips, is the taste of the body. This taste ripples through my cells, recognition: in this vastness I am minuscule, a fleshy pod inside a larger, sensing presence.

I dive toward the grassy bottom. Kelp beds sway with the shifting current like those fields of wheat in the Song of Songs, and my grandmother's voice reverberates. Long ago, she'd explained, the plains we walked upon were covered by water. There in my hand was the evidence, the signatures of shellfish embossed in stone.

Where is my basin now? Where those creatures whose stone imprints I found lodged in the mud of that pond? They have gone where I am going. I turn back toward shore and remember my hand reaching over my grandmother's pool, letting the twig go, watching it float on the water's tensile surface. Unschooled though I was in ceremony, I'd instinctively enacted rite. My act, like the priest's, was a bodily beseeching. *Pray, offer something alive.* I'd moved a bit of the scenery and read the consequences of my deed in the statement of falling rain.

In this linked cluster of events I understood my connection to the weave of experience we call the world. Now, beneath my feet, the bottom: water to fall into, land to stand on. Meanwhile the Ancient One, life giving death bringer, is always here. She conducts her ablutions ceaselessly, and, if we join her, takes us in.

Singer writes that she likes to imagine the earth as "an altar, a living one, that breathes." I emerge, taller, broader, my soul the shape of an unscathed sphere. I think of Rilke's ecstatic cry: *I am circling around God.* To embody transcendence is why we are here.

II.

The Sestina

Sacred and Profane

The Sestina as Rite

A high school English teacher assigned Dylan Thomas' villanelle "Do Not Go Gentle into That Good Night." I'd lost the hearing in my left ear when I was ten, and the poem drew me by its probing of loss. The villanelle rocked like a canoe on the buoyancy of diction and syntax, its two repeating lines the canoe's curved sides. "Poetry is a form, reaching out," Edward Hirsch writes, "a disembodied hand—a voice—coming from darkness into light. . . ."[1] Thomas' poem beckoned, and I used it as a model for my first villanelle.

Form became a fascination. At university I studied Auden's sestina "Paysage Moralise" and Pound's "Sestina: Altaforte," and the surrounding terrain: Ashbery, Bishop, Blumenthal, Hecht, Justice, Klappert, Kees, Lattimore, Meredith, McPherson, Van Duyn. Diane Wakoski was the first poet I heard read a sestina aloud. Later I was drawn to Marilyn Hacker's facility with form, and to her sestina "Toward Autumn." In Auden's "Paysage Moralise" the repeating teleutons were all nouns; ditto in "Toward Autumn"—*daughter, friend, bread, mother, lover, myself.* Additional repetitions of *friend* and *mother* within lines complicated and deepened the poem's musical range. The difficult fourth stanza failed to sag, but built and bridged into stanza five. And five lifted partly because Hacker enacts another repetition within the line (the word *women*)—adding that tactic's contrapuntal, emphatic energy.

> . . . To have a friend
> a generation older than myself

is sometimes like a letter for my daughter
to read, when she can read: What your mother

left undone, women who are not your mother
may do. Women who are not your lover
love you . . .

Reading sestinas, I felt myself present at the enactment of mysterious rite. The form itself felt freighted, but how? Was it that the sestina's design delivered the complementary pleasure of repetition and variation which Robert Hass elucidates in *Twentieth Century Pleasures*?

> . . . repetition initiates a sense of order. The feeling of magic comes from the way it puts us in touch with the promises of a deep sympathetic power in things: heart-beat, sunrise, summer solstice. . . . In the same way, freedom from pattern offers us at first an openness . . . and it contains the threat of chaos, rudderlessness, vacuity. Safety and magic on one side, freedom and movement on the other. . . .[2]

The two polarities are poetry's givens, and the sestina's repeating teleutons seem especially suited to deliver repetition and variation's pleasures. I think of Helen Frost's young adult novel in sestinas, *Keesha's House*, much celebrated by its wide readership: an impressive instance of the teleutons' rendering of these complementary staples of poetry. The teleutons rhyme with themselves, and as they float by, they take their place in the past, but they also reverberate forward, differently this time, since the present toward which they reverberate is not the same present in which they occurred. The repeating teleuton is each time itself, but each repetition takes place in changed scenery. As James Cummins notes, "the teleutons of the fifth stanza are not the teleutons of the first, though they hang the same way over the bridge-rail."[3]

And the chiming teleutons' power gets modernized in our era by variation. Two examples complement each other: Miller Williams' "The Shrinking Lonesome Sestina" and Jonah Winter's "Sestina: Bob." In Williams' poem the six teleutons alone constitute the sixth stanza.

Time
goes
too
fast.
Come
home.

In Winter's poem, all thirty-six lines end with the name of the narrator's rival, that most middle American of proper nouns: Bob.

According to her housemate, she is out with Bob
tonight, and when she's out with Bob
you never know when she'll get in. Bob
is an English professor. Bob
used to be in a motorcycle gang, or something, or maybe
  Bob
rides a motorcycle now. How radical of you, Bob—

Bob: the very sound suggests a dud, and there it is in the jilted lover's mouth, six times in each strophe, six in the *tornada.* Then there is the variation of the teleutons themselves. Arguments as to whether or not the teleutons should be varied are moot: it's happening. In Renée Ashley's "The Light, The Dark, The One Stone, And the Bird Looking On," *long* becomes *prolong, altar* becomes *alter, alteration.* Also inventive is Dan Bellm's "Book of Maps" in which the teleuton *boy* alternates three times with *girl,* and in the envoy (referred to in the sestina as the *tornada)* becomes *girlboy.* And the daring of outright substitution of teleutons ups the complexity quotient. In Lynn Domina's "Thursday"—a modern take on the psychological ambience of Christ's Last Supper—five teleutons are the names of Christ's disciples. The sixth is also, but in each stanza this sixth name changes.

The more I wrote and studied the sestina, the more I suspected that it wasn't simply a concentration of repetition and variation that drew readers and writers, but the fact of this concentration coupled with the sestina form. Focusing on the sestina's prosodic rationale, David Rothman writes that "those ends words that were furthest apart in any one stanza are placed as close as possible in the next," creating "the greatest possible sequential displacement and juxtaposition."[4] Robin Becker's "Sad Sestina" from *The Horse Fair* illustrates.

Sad Sestina

For Susanna Kaysen

Today's sadness is different from yesterday's:
more green in it, some light rain, premonition of departures
and the unpacking of books and papers. *It's not a bad thing*
to be sad, my friend Susanna says. *Go with it.* I'm going by foot
into this sadness, the way we go as children into the awful
school day and the hours of cruelty and misunderstanding,

the way we go into family, into the savagery of standing
up for ourselves among siblings and parents, in yesterday's
living room, where secrecy turns to habit and we learn the
awful,
unthinkable fact: time twists our days into a series of
departures.
When he was mad, my father used to say Someone's *got to foot*
the bills, and I think of him now, this man who knew one
thing

for sure: you had to pay your own way, since nothing
came free in this life. A young dyke, grandstanding
before the relatives, I held my sadness close, one foot
already out the door. Who could believe in yesterday's
homilies while women cruised me, seventeen and hot for
departure?
Today's sadness unfurls without drama, without the awful

punishments or reprisals of that house. In its place, the
awful,
simple, mystery of human melancholy. Most days, I'd trade
anything
to be rid of the blues, accustomed to flight and departure,
strategies that saved my life. Today I'm befriending it,
standing

beside my sadness like a pal down on her luck, who knows yesterday
isn't always a good predictor for tomorrow. A rabbit's foot

won't help; when the time comes, it's a question of putting my foot
in the stirrup and riding the sad horse of my body to the awful
little stable at the edge of town. And there to wait while yesterday
has its way with time. Susanna said, *To be sad is not a bad thing,*
and I believe her, as I pull the heavy saddle from the standing
horse and hang the bridle away. Sadness readies for my departure,

and I for hers. In a most unlikely departure
from the ordinary, even the tough butch on a bike will be a tenderfoot
when it comes to goodbyes. We carry on, notwithstanding
all the good times gone and December's awful
cheerfulness. Susanna, if I ever discern something
useful about sadness, I'll wish I'd known it yesterday.

I've put distracting things aside and discovered, underfoot,
no wisdom absent yesterday. Still, a saint would find this awful:
a standing date with change, a season of departures.

Thing ends line three in the first stanza and doesn't reappear until eight lines later, at the end of stanza two. Then it's repeated almost immediately at the end of the first line of stanza three—this immediate repetition heightened by Becker's variation, moving from the amorphousness of *thing* to the absolute of *nothing.* Then this teleuton doesn't appear again until a full seven lines later, at which point the absolute *nothing* becomes *anything.* This pattern of repeating recurs with the other five teleutons. Now furthest apart, now cheek by jowl, now apart again. The teleutons enact polar extremes of positioning—first far apart, then close—linked into a dyad by repetition. I'm reminded of

Buddhism's perception that the appearance of phenomena is dyadic—phenomena "rise up" and "pass away." The ardent writer of sestinas James Cummins also perceives this movement from one pole to the other and refers to it as "the voyage out, the return . . . . ."[5] The sestina's encoding of this pattern of polar moments linked by repeating teleutons fuels a peculiarly intoxicating tension.

"Sad Sestina" is instructive in that the speaker's underlying ambivalence toward the subject of sadness echoes the form's dyadic *no* and *yes, gone* then *here.* Sadness has a way of seeming maddeningly even and unaccented at the same time that we experience it as painful. In "Sad Sestina" a level tone is underscored by the fact that there are no end-stopped lines until just before the *tournada.* This levelness is further underscored by insistently recurring repetitions within lines of the words *sad* and *sadness.* The name *Susanna* is also repeated, echoing that same vowel and sibilant. Sadness: the repeated aural intoning of that vowel wrapped in the soft swish of *s* sounds suggests the poet steeping herself in sadness the way one steeps herbs for tea. And indeed she states that she's "befriending" sadness. But the poem's negotiation of this emotion feels painful and concludes that even "a saint would find this awful." We sense that the speaker wants to push the emotion away at the same time that she entertains it. Thus the yes and no dynamic of ambivalence in subject matter mirrors the dyadic movement in the form.

"The sestina," Cummins writes, referring to the medieval period, "is a relic from an age of faith."[6] The verb *Trobar* means to invent and compose verse. The Troubadour poet Arnaut Daniel is credited with inventing the sestina. In his form the forward pattern of teleutons ending the six lines of the first stanza is altered in the following stanza in a way that suggests a braid. As the braider crosses the strand in the center with a strand from the left, then from the right, so Daniel took the teleuton from the top and then the one from the bottom and places them side by side in the second stanza, repeating this three times, working from the top and bottom lines inward. He called this pattern the *retrogradatio cruciata. Retrogradatio* (from medieval Latin) refers to backward movement, and *cruciata* (from *crux,* meaning cross) implies crossing. Thus the term might loosely be rendered as "backward crossing" or "crossing backward."

Troubadour poets understood that writing and reciting poems was a way of mediating desire within time's flux. In this process one gained a sense of "self-knowledge and completion from the experience of loving, composing and singing viewed as an inseparable unity."[7] They composed in an era when Pythagorean number theory was in vogue, and Daniel would have known that the number six represented the highest state of union attainable in the profane world. Six, the lowest multiple of three and two, appears in geometry as the double triangle. This double triangle—Seal of Solomon, star of David—corresponded to the middle sephiroth of the Kaballah tree, the sephiroth which joins heaven and earth—top and bottom of the tree—to its male and female left and right. Six represented the "perfect marriage" of polar opposites in earthly life and temporal time. And the number six, Marianne Shapiro writes, was considered the numerical equivalent of perfect harmony wherein one might hear the music of the spheres.[8]

The sestina foregrounds this charged number. Six stanzas of six lines each, followed by the envoy or *tornada* in which the six teleutons appear again in their original order. If we assign numbers one through six to the teleutons in the sestina's first strophe, the method for determining the order of the following strophe is a pincer pattern shifting from the outer lines toward the center. The order in strophe one appears in stanza two as 6 1, 5 2, 4 3. This new pattern combines a triadic component and a dyadic one: three sets of pairs. The original order from strophe one appears now as two triads of alternating numbers: 1 2 3 (alternating with 6 5 4) hold to their original order, whereas the 4 5 6 triad is now in reverse order. Thus the pattern, three pairs of two numbers simultaneously unfolding in reverse order (6 and 1, 5 and 2, 4 and 3). We "braid backward," arrive at the centerless center, and pause—stanza break—then begin again. When we arrive at the end of the 36 lines, we have exhausted this pattern's possibilities.

Now to "closure" and "resolution." Six times we've come to numerology's "perfect marriage" in profane time. But six lacks what Shapiro calls a center.

> When the order of rhyme-words has progressed in a pincer movement of 6 1 5 2 4 3, having reached the last two terms, the pincer movement closes upon nothing. The rhyme-word 3 is underscored by repetition in the first line of the next strophe, but this emphasis . . . serves only to indicate the generation of a new, centerless strophe.[9]

Mircea Eliade's studies of myth and religion describe the "center" as an *axis mundi* or earthly location where sacred and material worlds meet. There we transcend linear time and enter eternal time—a sphere, Eliade asserts, where we may experience space, the world and consciousness as divine. Shapiro believes the sestina embodies this leap from the physical world into the divine center in two ways. First, the head-tailed linking of strophes (where the last teleuton of one strophe repeats as the first teleuton of the next) suggests the tail-biting serpent Uroboros, a figure for cyclic regeneration; and second, the pairing of teleutons in three sets, 6 and 1, 5 and 2, 4 and 3, which yields in each case the sum of seven. Numbers one through six corresponded to geometric forms and the material world, but seven was formless. Formless because it represented the marriage of dyadic opposites embodied in the number six now elevated into the spiritual realm. Eliade cites Philo Judaeus' interpretation of the six days of creation after which, on the seventh day, God rested, opening profane, earthly existence into eternal, "timeless" time.

"In numerology," Shapiro writes, seven "is the number of eternity and mutability, of the temporal, sublunary world and the world of the eternal Sabbath."[10] The pairing of lines in the backward braiding results three times in each stanza in a sum of seven. We have fleetingly experienced three times in each stanza Shapiro's leap from profane to sacred time.

Cummins thinks we may have "lost the meaning of the number mysticism that the medieval mind associated with the sestina" and concludes that we must "somehow feel their meaning in the poem."[11] We can. The poet John Frederick Nims writes that we "are affected by precise relationships we are not conscious of."[12] He argues that we "feel" meaning in the same way that we perceive without being aware of them the Golden Section's "golden numbers" or the Fibonacci sequence when we see it in plants. In similar fashion the symbolism of six and seven resonate subliminally when we hear them in a poem.

Within the thirty-six instances of the teleutons, each stanza brings forth three pairs of numbered lines, the sum of which is seven. The form delivers eighteen instances of the number seven *in situ.* We see, Cummins writes, "the sense of circularity and completion—of Eliade's sacred and profane time—that resonated in the medieval mind, and resonates still."[13]

I've suggested that the *retrogradatio cruciata*'s dyadic movement enacts a cathartic rite. Yes—yes but—and then again yes. In a general sense all poems might be said to deliver some version of transcendent feeling. Every poem mediates time, flashing its repetition and variation, performing itself through duration. A poem makes time interesting. But the unique gestalt of the *retrogradatio cruciata,* Cummins argues, turns this mediation on time into a structural component of the form, which "self-consciously calls attention to its [the sestina's] existence-in-time."[14] Think of duration as a sensuous arena in which our human sense of diurnal time varies and may sometimes seem to extend expansively. We feel, often enough, immortal, for a while. But the *retrogradatio cruciata*'s delivery of effects which depend on counterpointing long against short duration is unique and uniquely suited to deliver its effect.

Examine in "Sad Sestina" the progression of the teleuton *foot.* "I'm going by foot / into this sadness," Becker writes in stanza one, introducing the theme of time. To go by foot suggests not the thrill of speed but its opposite. The fact of "going by foot" implies that the speaker anticipates that this encounter with sadness will move slowly. The vowel sound stopped by a *t* resembles the treading thud of a single step. It counterpoints the sibilant *s* sounds of *sad, sadness* and *Susanna.* Both aurally and by its meaning "going by foot" underscores the fact that the poet will entertain sadness for a good while.

In stanza two *foot* becomes a verb in the father's remark that "someone's got to foot / the bills." Calling up the harrowing of family conflict begins to intensify discomfort, and inevitably we register again *foot*'s first appearance as a description of the laborious moment-by-moment way that this journey through time will take place. In stanza three tension around progress through time twists tighter as the speaker, now claiming the label *dyke*, has "one foot / already out the door." One foot—not two. That recognition again throws us back to *foot*'s first two unsettling contexts. These contexts now reverberate and are intensified by this smidgen of qualified hope: one foot out the door, but only one.

Stanza three begins the *retrogradatio cruciata*'s pyrotechnics. *Foot* ends line three, and a stanza and a half pass before *foot* closes stanza four. In stanza five it occurs just one line later. Far apart, then close. In stanza four the fact that "a rabbit's foot / won't help" counters the momentary hope of escape raised in stanza three and re-invokes the sense of time as plodding. It echoes the dolor of the previous instances and loads on more. The baggage of sadness weighs heavily now. And stanza five's "foot / in the stirrup" is no lift, since the rider approaches the "awful / stable . . . ." But at the same time "foot / in the stirrup," occurring just one line after the rabbit's foot—that word again, so soon—jolts us. The spatially close teleutons' rhyming acts like a spurt of adrenaline in the blood. Far, then close. Fading, then reasserting themselves anew.

Now the poem progresses seven full lines rather than six before *foot* sounds again. Add to this the fact that we experience this sounding while also experiencing the complex matrix of five other teleutons in their process of acting out exactly this pattern.

Through stanza five the duration of sadness has felt heavily freighted. But the use of *foot* in stanza six introduces into the poem's context a surprising turn. The speaker's sense of herself as tough dyke takes on nuance: she's also a *tenderfoot*. In this new incarnation the reverberation of the first five instances—emphatically loaded with angst—springs up, as though embossed in relief. The speaker delineates this moment in time as one of high irony: even parting from sadness, it seems, may feel momentarily sad. This startling perception inevitably calls up all the previous instances of *foot* and reverberates both with and against them. What seemed a fixed trajectory, we're reminded, changes. "Sad Sestina" demonstrates eloquently that it's flux which truly characterizes duration: how amazingly things can and do change through time—even as things may seem to our ploddingly habitual minds to remain the same.

In life's shifting landscape, the sestina suggests, we can find no absolute. Thus we welcome any transcendent moments we can get, however momentary. When this occurs, we may know, briefly, that state of being which Marianne Shapiro calls "the erotic abandonment of reason," meaning the dissolving of a fixed self, and "surrender . . . to the movements of sun and moon . . . telling and retelling myths of soul, immortality, and rebirth."[15] The key to the sestina's allure is this rhythmic experience of linear time in which, for moments at a time, we feel jolted beyond it.

I suggested that Becker's content renders the speaker's yes and no ambivalence. We can say that previous utterances of the teleuton inform each present instance with the knowledge of its own history, at the same time that this history is transformed and enlarged by each present instance. The past reverberates in the present. Thus each teleuton contains "more, or other than its previous incarnation, while it contains its own echo."[16] Eighteen times we're brought from profane time into cyclic time, and for that duration we may experience intimations of immortality. Then, "simultaneously and decisively," Shapiro notes, "the event of the poem leaves us an open door."[17]

That door opening from cyclic back into linear time is the *tornada*. We might at first imagine it as the sestina's final cathartic pinnacle. And indeed repetition, confined in a small space, intensifies. The teleutons, having performed their ardent roles, gather on stage to take that final bow—as though saying *this is about to be over, but you won't be the same now, not by any measure.* But this envoy is no ordinary summary. It puts an end to the cyclic character of the six strophes and opens the door back into quotidian time. And the teleutons underscore this. Their original order in stanza one is now reiterated. What time is it? Time to return to the daily round.

The teleutons in the *tornada* reel off quickly, stressing the fact that they, and we, are fleeting. But suppose that we resist time's passing and long to postpone closure. There are ways to engage and withdraw, to play and extend play. For example, a double sestina capped by one *tornada.* Or we may resist the *tornada*'s lock by writing an "open ended" sestina capped with a single line of *"tornado"*—if such flagrant disregard of the pattern is urged by the poem's content. Or we may emphasize the poignant nature of longing as does Marie Ponsot, who wrestles with our pre-occupation with impermanence in "Half Life: Copies To All Concerned." Though she's used the six teleutons in the *tornada,* she adds a final line which reiterates all six.

> I should say, as well: beyond what I ask
> Lies the you you lost alive; in my thought
> Still planning to be good. Redeem him now.
> Now ask your thought for this lost good. Farewell.

The *tornada,* followed by that emphatic, extra line, doubles the sense of finality at the same time that the final line sneaks in one last riff of longing. It insists—as though to underscore our desire for an absolute closure life doesn't deliver—until it's over. Shapiro puts this in prosodic terms.

> Cyclical movement and movement that is directed toward a formal end contend with one another in the sestina so that the formal dismissal in the tornada nevertheless betrays an open ended doubt, tentativeness, or rejection of the absolute and unqualified assertion.[18]

The sestina allows us to wear ethereal lineaments—briefly—and then it's back to growing older. In Becker's *tornada,* the seventh and final instance of *foot* brings the experience of hanging out with sadness back to the beginning. Befriending sadness has delivered no new knowledge. The speaker finds "underfoot / no wisdom absent yesterday" and concludes by invoking the specter of our "standing date with change." Sadness endures, until it doesn't (just like everything else), and will surely recur.

Hanging out with sadness for the duration might or might not deliver transcendence. Hanging out with "Sad Sestina" just may do the trick, because the *retrogradatio cruciata*'s symbolic structure delivers, and because "Sad Sestina" returns us to what we knew all along. You can step out of the river for a while, but then you'll step back in. Becker's *tornada* constitutes one last re-iteration of the plight of duration: we who long for permanence are fatally impermanent—and mortal.

Notes

1. Edward Hirsch, "Beyond Desolation," *American Poetry Review,* May/June 1997, p. 33.
2. Robert Hass, *Twentieth Century Pleasures* (New York:The Echo Press, 1984), p. 216–17.
3. James Cummins, "Calliope Music: Notes on the Sestina," *American Poet,* fall 1997, p. 33.
4. David J. Rothman, "An Enchanted Realm of Endless Transformations: Sestina Form and the Retrogradatio Cruciata," *Hellos,* Vol. 2, No. 2, 1991, p. 307.
5. Cummins, op. cit., p. 33.
6. Ibid.
7. *New Princeton Encyclopedia of Poetry and Poetics,* , Alex Preminger and T. V. F. Brogan, editors (Princeton University Press, 1993), p. 845.
8. Marianne Shapiro, *Hieroglyph of Time: The Petrarchan Sestina* (Minneapolis: University of Minnesota Press, 1980), p. 13.
9. Ibid.
10. Ibid.
11. Cummins, op. cit, p. 31.
12. John Frederick Nims, *Western Wind* (New York: Random House, 1983), p. 315.
13. Cummins, op. cit., p. 33.
14. Ibid., p. 32.
15. Shapiro, op. cit., p. 163.
16. Cummins, op. cit., p. 33.
17. Shapiro, op. cit, p. 164.
18. Shapiro, op. cit., p. 19.

Ardor and the Sestina

In *Poetry: The Unsayable Said* Donald Hall suggests that poems deliver intense emotion we hadn't expected. We feel bodily pleasure, fulfillment, contentment, uncountable versions of deep satisfaction and a sense of "rightness beyond reason." This happens because a lyric poem's sound effects overshadow mere meaning. The sonic realm takes over, and sound powers the poet's argument. I call this intensity the lyric produces in the perceiver *ardor,* a word from ME and OFr, meaning flame or fire, and Latin's *ardere* "to burn." I want poems that deliver this fire. If there is no ardor, I may as well read a newspaper. As the dancer Isadora Duncan succinctly said, *All art is religious, or else it is mere merchandise.*

My search for ardor led me to the sestina and its presumed creator Arnaut Daniel. In the medieval era Pythagorean numerology was in vogue, and six, the lowest multiple of three and two, appeared in geometry as the double triangle. In numerology, six was believed to represent the "perfect marriage" of polar opposites in temporal time. Daniel would have been acquainted with numerology, and would have known that the number six stood for the highest state of being in the profane world. The sestina we believe he invented is composed of six stanzas of six lines each, in which the last word in each line repeats in each subsequent stanza in a prescribed order.

To heighten the poem's closure, he added a three-line envoy in which the six teleutons appear in their original order for a *seventh* time—this time much closer together, two teleutons in each of the envoy's three lines. In numerology seven represented a transcendent leap from the earthy world onto the spiritual plane. To hear the teleutons sound a seventh time was to experience transcendence.

Mythic insinuations of transcendence may or may not signify. For like any other poem, the sestina depends not only on its formal shape and size, but also on all of poetry's other lyric devices. A literary dictionary's definition of rhyme—the similarity of words' sounds—offers a dozen differing variations of rhyme. Prominent among these, for instance, are assonance—recurring vowel sounds in stressed syllables, as in "twinkle, twinkle, little star / how I wonder what you are"—and consonance, the repetition of consonants as in *hill* and *hall.*

Another prominent consideration is rhythm, a boat floating the hearer through time. Rhythm is composed of repetition and variation. In *September 1, 1939,* for instance, Auden varied the three-foot tetrameter lines now and again with a four-foot line. *I and the public know / What all schoolchildren learn, / Those to whom evil is done / Do evil in return.* Repetitions and variations go straight to our hearts, then spread through our sensitive bodies on waves of pleasurable satisfaction.

I won't argue that the sestina delivers more bang for its buck than other formal lyrics. Nor will I argue that a form such as the sestina will necessarily deliver the passionate utterance I'm calling *ardor.* For whether a poem delivers ardor ultimately depends on the writer. It's the writer who tips the balance toward ardor or away.

James Cummins: The Voice of the Lyricist

Cummins, who teaches at the University of Cincinnati and curates the Elliston Poetry Collection, may have written more sestinas than any other American poet. In his latest collection, *Still Some Cake,* his skill is evident in a sestina entitled "Tiresias."

Cummins evokes blind Tiresias who lived seven years in a woman's body, then zooms in on the dynamics of the nuclear family, and the concept—complex and ever-shifting—of gender.

> You learn how to be a man from your father.
> Your mother teaches you how to be a woman.
> You have to be afraid of becoming an old man
> before you'll take on the wiles of the mother—

her movements, gestures, the way her face
suddenly, at odd moments, becomes your face.

A crucial part of Cummins' art is his choice of teleutons. A less accomplished poet might choose either the word *woman* or *mother,* and either *man* or *father* as repeating teleutons, but not both. Cummins chooses both because repetition is one of poetry's base constants, and because as a general rule, the more repetition and variation in a single poem, the better.

Then he goes further and chooses the word *face* as not one but two of the six teleutons, thus *doubling* the repetition of the word's sounding in this first and all subsequent stanzas. He has loaded the teleutons with more musical wattage than any other sestina I know.

Also the word *face* has the advantage of serving as both a noun and a verb. A generous amount of ardor is built into the poem automatically by this skilled choice of two directly rhyming (i.e., repeating) teleutons.

Another crucial decision is Cummins' choice of the second person, genderless *you* voice for his poem's narration. The advantages of second person are:

1. *You* speaks with neutrality for all genders.
2. *You* automatically infuses the poem with frequent, ongoing, direct rhyme.
3. *You* directly and repeatedly solicits and includes the listener/reader.
4. *You* serves as the neutral voice of a teacher who knows his subject.

The poem begins:

Turns out that old adage about saving face
was really about saving the face of the father.
His was the look you wanted on your face
whenever you'd realize you were a woman.
Those moments shocked you—and your mother,
who'd assumed you'd turn out to be a man.

This is a poem, says the poet Denise Duhamel, "in which identity is intentionally blurred, disguised, and traded." To take on this issue, Cummins takes the stance of a wise lecturer with a wry sense of humor. In the stanza above, the final two lines are amusing, and they urge those in the audience, for the time being, to hold judgment in abeyance.

I'm compelled by the sounding of the word *face* repeating three times. *Face* is also rhymed with *saving*, and *woman* rhymed with *man*. There is the direct rhyme of *you* with *you* and there is iambic pentameter's rhythm that soothes us and suggests that the poem will unfold effortlessly, like a boat slowly drifting on the water of a stream.

> But it's not that you haven't ended up a man.
> Mornings you shave, staring into a man's face.
> You have the proper attitude toward your mother.
> You just don't want to be a man like your father,
> and the best way to do that is to be a woman.

This is a confessional poem in the best sense of that word. In a culture where conscious self-knowledge is the exception, we hear, in Cummins' confidence, a man who knows himself thoroughly. And with that bit of humor in the fourth and fifth lines, this narrator wins his listeners' trust. End-stopped lines and sentences linked by a comma preponderate, suggesting that we are students relearning attitudes toward gender at the hands of an accomplished instructor. We are secure beside him in his lazily drifting boat.

In the last line of the stanza, the speaker plunges us into a dramatic scene which continues into stanzas four and five.

> The first time you saw this happen in your face,
>
> it scared you—your hand flew up to your face.
> Not only did you have the cunning of a man,
> but now you also had the guile of a woman.
> You look into the mirror at your new face,
> the one begun the night you surprised your father,
> humping a blanket that turned into your mother.

How could the bastard do that to your mother?
And why had you never seen this in her face?
What was it you saw the next day in your father?
A look that told you he was the better man?
And what do you think he saw in your face?
Did he know then that you were a woman?

The drama implicit in the fourth stanza turns us from statements about gender to a scene played out with consequences. The six lines, each end-stopped with a question mark, toll through the drama, and we feel ourselves as male and female at once: we are human beings. As though to reinforce this perception, in the stanza before the envoy the two teleutons *face* appear side by side in the center of the stanza.

You repressed that morning in the way a woman
might repress an impractical love for a man.
When he's around, you can see it in her face—
her Don't-trust-him-but-still-love-him face.
Your father never thought of you as a man.
It was natural you'd try to seduce your father.

The envoy, with its gently humorous final line, is in keeping with the tone of the wise teacher delivering his summation.

First you showed your father your "mother" face;
but then you showed him your other face,
the sly face a man wears when he's a woman.

Cummins' command of the sestina form is as impressive as it is unobtrusive. I come away reluctantly, filled by the plethora of lyric soundings, steeped in Cummins' skillful use of poetry's musical attributes. With his ability to create, deepen, expand and intensify this sestina's ardor, he has delivered.

Patricia Smith: The Voice of the Wound and Its Survivor

The world of Spoken Word poetry powers the poet Patricia Smith—or perhaps it's Patricia Smith who has powered Spoken

Word poetry onto the world stage. Among the sestinas she has written in *Blood Dazzler* and other venues is a sestina featuring Stevie Wonder as protagonist. Let its long, fraught lines enter you.

Looking to See How the Eyes
Inhabit Dark, Wondering about Light

In December 1999, Stevie Wonder sought to undergo an operation to partially restore his sight. He made the round of talk shows, trumpeting the possibilities. Then the story dropped off the radar. Doctors declared he was not a good candidate for the procedure.

Look. When he assumes he is alone, he absently claws the air
  for light.
See how he pulls the sun toward himself. Even as he
  conjures, wonders,
eyes spit their cruel blanks, drench him in mud. His mama is
  the dark;
dark is his daddy. A shiver in his lids becomes his next
  church, his eyes
wonder at the black bottomless flash, the siphoning of
  narrative. He can see
light as it exists in memory—lush, fleeting, then maddening.
  Made ya look.

The poem's first word is a single statement. *Look.* To whom is it addressed? To Wonder himself? To we who read Smith's poem? The word reverberates with irony, for to look is precisely what Stevie Wonder cannot do. But the word is italicized, and we will encounter it again as one of Smith's teleutons. Her decision was a musical, compositional decision, rather like Cummins'. She understands the power of repetition and the sense of anchorage it delivers. Her choice is also smart because the word *wonder* here is a famous name and also a verb *and* a noun. Like Cummins, Smith has chosen teleutons that offer not only themselves, but also the slant rhyme of *look,* and *dark,* the alliteration of *look* and *light.* She has smartly built a hefty amount of compelling repetition and rhyme into the poem's structure.

The first line renders the angst and loneliness of the wounded one longing to be whole. The verb *claws* resonates with a sense of urgency in the face of helplessness. In the second line—see how he pulls the sun toward himself—the alliteration of *see* and *sun* and *himself* comforts us with these repetitions. That same line repeats *conjures* and *wonders,* words like a gentle hand stroking our backs. And at stanza's end we are again reassured by the repetition of *fleeting* and *maddening.*

In the second stanza notice the similar sounds of *tongue* and *wonder* and *answer* and *finger.* Notice *lid* and *orb.*

Darkness strives to be his comfort. But he is obsessed by the
 need to look,
eyes flat, roiling, his head adjusting as if. He tilts toward each
 tongue of light,
wonders at its evil sweet, squints, strains. Dark whispers, if
 you must see,
see the gifts I have given—the unflinching knowledge of self,
 the wild wonder
light has birthed in you, how it blooms without answer. He
 touches his eye.
Look. He lifts the lid, pokes the dead orb with a finger, cries
 out again to dark.

Stanza three offers the constellation of *clock, dark* and *look.* Smith describes his eyes "clawing for light." She calls our attention to "look how completely he has learned the language of the hand" with which he covers blind eyes, "wanting to see."

Seasons change only on his skin. Chill and steam nudge the
 edges of dark.
Wondering what year, what June, what clock it is, his useless
 eyes look,
light upon layered shadow, scan the unraveled empty. He
 curses those eyes,
eyes that simply loll and water and grow impossibly wide,
 clawing for light.
Look how completely he has learned the language of the
 hand, stark wonder
darkening weary palms as he presses them flat against
 against, wanting to see.

In the fourth stanza Smith invokes doctors who hold out bits of hope. Tension builds as "doctors tout the shattered dark, / look beneath trembling lids for doors, promise his child's face." Smith then recounts the shattering of this dream, the end of the final line of that stanza "how he weeps for eyes."

> Eyes, they say, can be sexed, propped wide, flooded with
> daybreak. He'll see
> lightning, dim dance, maybe a minute of day. Doctors tout
> the shattered dark,
> look beneath trembling lids for doors, promise his child's
> face. And he wonders—
> wonder being the only response he trusts—as hope is
> unleashed. It hurts to look.
> Dark, desperately clutching, woos him, redefines beauty as
> the absence of light.
> See his torso ripple, how he fights with his own fingers, how
> he weeps for eyes.

In stanza five she shakes up the ante by taking to task "the religious who whisper the promise of eyes" and asks when these religious figures will realize that dark "owns him." In our materialist culture of acquisition, the verb *owns* registers as a heartbreaking truth. Thus the end of the fifth stanza's fifth line is blunt. Now that he realizes there is no available cure, Smith tells us how he feels: *It hurts to look.* It hurts to look, and then the end of the sixth line ironically replies: *It's much safer to wonder.*

> Light is overrated, they decide. Best not to shock the system,
> rip holes in the dark,
> see up close the cacophonous stanzas sight scribbles over
> time. It hurts to look.
> Eyes overwork, tangle lessons best learned by touch. It's
> much safer to wonder.

Now that Stevie Wonder realizes there is no cure, Smith tells us how he feels: *It hurts to look.* The end of the sixth line ironically replies: *It's much safer to wonder.* The two short sentences brings us up short. Get it, these lines say. He will never see.

Light a match, wave it back and forth, watch him follow the
waltzing heat. Wonder,
darkly, what hollow blessings he has left to cling to. He
follows music with his eyes,
sees the notes rollick black upon black. He snakes his
balding head, pretends to look,
looking like a man who has never watched another man
move. Now it's easy to see—
eyes would ruin him. Shadow puppets have answered every
question. The dark,
wonderful, forgiving, takes his hand and leads him, like a
lover, away from the light.

Smith's unusually long lines foreswear the obedience of iambic pentameter. She wisely senses that the shape and heft of this sestina's subject calls for more: more words, more length, more weight, more room and more time—time to sing longer, time to expand the poem in whatever way each moment of composition demands. The sixth stanza begins with the word *light.* And the word *light,* also one of the teleutons, is the teleuton that ends this stanza. How's that for music!

Now comes the envoy. Why has Smith set off the envoy by rendering it in italics? Why shrink the envoy's three lines to two? Because Wonder's sight is dwindling?

Light simply makes us wonder and crave the dark.
I've seen how desperately you look for me.

In the first line all of "us" calls up the hearer of the poem. We who are not blind take light for granted. Is it Smith herself who utters the final line of the envoy, speaking directly to Stevie Wonder? *I've seen how desperately you look for me.* Smith would make common cause with Wonder, and does. By sestina's end we know we're in the hands of a gifted poet. May her revealed music and her hidden music go on speaking.

Destruction and the Blossom

The Sestina in War

I passed through Colombo's burgeoning, green paradise in April, the hottest month, when the Plumeria trees' blossoms were loosening their sweetness into the air. Children picked up the fallen flowers and sniffed the perfume, and so did I. While old men squatted and smoked cigarettes in the shade of a tobacco shop's roof, and harried mothers and fathers with a child by each hand walked to the bus stop, soldiers with rifles paced back and forth on the sidewalk. The blossoms seemed an instance of beauty nothing could damage, but might this be the day a Tamil Tiger suicide bomber walked calmly into that tobacco shop?

I am a writer, and writing sestinas had become my default. When I travel, the sestina form's thirty-nine-line structure comes with me like my tooth brush. The words at the end of the first six lines repeat six more times in the remaining five six-line stanzas and the three-line envoy. Each stanza's repeating words are called teleutons, and in each successive stanza the teleutons appear at the ends of the lines again, *but in a new, prescribed order.*

By the end of the sixth stanza, all six teleutons have appeared once in all of the lines, and they will appear again one last time in the three-line envoy. But the teleutons are not simply repeating. Each teleuton is repeating in an entirely new context.

The day after I arrived there came to me two contrasting images: *Scent of Plumeria, and the smell of burning.* Several years earlier anti-Tamil riots had flared in Colombo, and the smell of smoke called up those riots and the burning rubber tire "necklaces" thrown over an adversary's head. That phrase became the first line of the sestina, and a second line elaborated and replied to the first. *Not one or the other, but both. Destruction, and the blossom.* For several days I carried these two lines with me, listening to their wisdom resound in my mind.

Warscape with Lovers

Scent of Plumeria, and the smell of burning.
Not one or the other, but both. Destruction, and the
    blossom.
Sweetheart, I'm afraid. That boy with the rifle breaks
the catechism in two. And in two. Let me
see us whole, beside the sea. My body
busy, paying attention to yours. Already. . . .

The two first lines were imagistic seeds. The third line presented a woman addressing her lover. "Sweetheart, I'm afraid." She offers an image of a boy with a rifle blasting wholeness to pieces, then mitigates this with an image of herself and her lover whole "beside the sea," a tranquil, safe setting. But of course. The antidote to war is love. It's destruction and the blossom again, those two complementary images that will repeat in each stanza.

But image alone does not produce poetry. Pause and focus on the words' sounds. The lines deliver four alliterating words: *burning, blossom, break* and *body.* These four words appear at the end of each of four of the sestina's lines, and become two thirds of the sestina's teleutons. The energy of alliteration fills space with the resounding *b* sound: *burning, blossom, breaking, body.* Is this *b* a sound my body longs for? Do we like the *b* sound because we live in bodies?

Repetition is soothing, and four of this sestina's teleutons begin with b. The last of the four is *body,* which suggests the rhyming word *already. Already* becomes the first stanza's final teleuton. *Already* announces that an event is over, or that some other event is imminent. Though I longed to feel safe and loved, I was in a place where things might change quickly without warning. I wanted to stroll the streets, but I often chose a taxi, imagining a taxi might be safer. Each time my driver approached a checkpoint, he pulled over and showed his ID. The soldier then glanced at me and waved us on. But the fact that we'd passed through a checkpoint without harm meant little. Colombo was a city in which it would be difficult to relax until the war was over.

In the second stanza the word *Already* signals hopefulness: perhaps the lovers' liaison will last, in spite of war's breakage. But halfway through the stanza, the lovers confront images of terror and admit that there is no safe haven.

> . . . Already
> we rock each other with our voices. Already
> we're braiding the invisible cord. That burning
> hut on T.V. isn't ours, but could be. My body
> could be hers, child at dead breast. That blossom
> of blood and bone could be your face. Let me
> say truth: no place, no one, is safe. The breaking . . .

I'd added to the anxiety yet more *b* words: *blood, bone* and *breast.* And though the word *already* suggests reassuring closeness between the lovers, the woman points out that *no place, no one, is safe.* Now I glance back to the first stanza's second line: *Not one or the other, but both. Destruction, and the blossom.* It was then that I understood: war highlights two alternating energies: love and destruction, beauty and ugliness, safety and vulnerability. Not one or the other, but both.

I walked out a bit before sunset, meditating on this dyad. Women strolled a market in saris, choosing slabs of fish. An ambulance siren swelled, then diminished. Does the soldier's left hand know what his right hand is thinking? A suicide bomber might wear a suit and tie like that banker. Fearful anxiousness described this city's ambiance, and I understood then that to convey the atmosphere of war in the capital, I would need to render all of the sestina's thirty-nine lines at the same high level of nervous uncertainty and anxious caution the populace had to live with 24/7. This was not the sestina's usual arc. But to render the air of threat was my task.

> . . . The breaking
> of vows, we know, is a given. Sweetheart, you'll break
> my heart. I've broken yours, but look: already
> you love me again. Destruction and the blossom: let me

> say it another way: that soldier, burning
> to become fabulous, torches the thatch (see blossomy
> flame) of the enemy's hospital: cut to my body. . . .

Are these alternating images of destruction and the blossom too predictably repetitive? The woman reveals that she and her lover have sworn vows and broken them, and that the making and breaking of vows is inevitable. Like that pair "destruction and the blossom," these two opposite energies are a fact of life. Thus in each stanza the same two energies manifest: war's hateful destruction, and the human blossom.

In Colombo there was not only war with Tamil Tigers, but another unofficial war between citizens and their government's death squads. In this beleaguered society you couldn't be sure of even your most intimate relationships. Your partner might fail you, you might fail your partner, and your government might turn on you as well.

I'd arrived shortly after the most violent episode to date. Suicide bombers had penetrated the financial district, damaged the Central Bank and its image of prosperity and power. The suicide bombers had murdered themselves, fifty-some citizens, and injured hundreds more.

Thus far the woman has managed war's relentless atmosphere of anxiety, but now this effort takes its toll. It's an attribute of the sestina form that emotional content builds toward the fourth stanza's rhythmic peak, and the woman now reaches that peak.

> . . . clay taking shape in your hands. Body by body,
> war piled on war: *when will the heart break*
> *all the way open?*

Her question is the poem's shimmering pivot.

> Thunder of mortar, blossom
> in the gutter. The soldier firing the mortar already
> dead. How we live: running from the burning
> field, into each other's arms. . . .

To break all the way open is to acknowledge our frailty and to fully inhabit the human condition. We feel her relief, and in the following stanza she articulates her acceptance of things as they are.

. . . Let me

lie along your side. Give me something to hold. Let me
ride those waves pouring from your fingers. The bodies
of the disappeared toll like bells. Our koan burns:
it cannot be solved. The whole and the broken,
dream and nightmare: your hand in my hair, already
familiar, could be the torturer's. Vase and its blossoms
camouflage for the bomb. . . .

The sestina's formal structure has elicited the breaking of her heart, and her admission frees us into a sacred, timeless pause, releasing us from fearful imagining into acceptance of *what is.*

Now she appreciates her wholeness and her own and her lover's deliverance. Thus the sestina concludes with gratitude.

. . . You love where you can. Blossom:
a thing of promise. That's us. Now: let me
let this go. Our glass, half full—already
there's more—swells toward the rim. Ours the bodies
the death squads passed by. The refugees make a break
for the fence, running for their lives, crossing this burning,

broken, blossoming Century. They've already
paid our dues. Sweetheart, let me show you how,
hand on the body's book, now swear the burning vow.

The woman is alive, and though neither she nor we know this war's outcome, in the arena of the sestina she has the last word. She urges her partner once more to swear a vow, and this time the vow is "burning." Will its flame bring these lovers conflagration or transformation?

Writing transforms the writer. It nudges and shifts us, ultimately profoundly changing our consciousness. I was no longer the woman I'd been a few days before. I had a distinct sense of writing's closure and completion, and I felt opened, lifted, expanded.

I went out and strolled slowly through the evening crowd. The perfume of the Plumeria blossoms surrounded me with sweetness, and I stood still, savoring that perfume. A mother walking with two children held each child by the hand, and two soldiers with rifles paced, watching evening shoppers. Women in front of a nearby shop bought bags of rice and dhal. Men in a truck delivering mangos to a stall hauled the fruit inside. I noted the nearby tobacco shop and the men squatting there, smoking. To negotiate the possibility of terror, you have to stay focused in the present, and that was what all of us there were trying to do.

III.

Litany

All Hail Litany

Three Variations

The repeating sound of water, the repeating whir of wind, animal shrieks. The planet's first sounds were not words but bird cries. The longing to bathe in sound and rhythm has been with us since the first humans gripped a stone in each hand and clapped the two stones together. Later someone stretched animal hide over a frame, made a drum. Later still, humans would have imitated these sounds and chanted them. Thus litany's repeating came into the world.

Through eons when we rose and walked out of the cave's dark into the beautiful, terrifying world, we looked for ways to comfort ourselves. We still respond to litany's primordial and endlessly repeating drum.

Repetition and Variation

The two forces that create poetry's "sonic singing" are repetition and variation. The recurring of sunrise and sunset soothes us, just as do repeating sounds and rhythms in music and poems. Repetition is grounding, reassuring, comforting—and then enough is enough, and we long for variation. Variation is an expanding outward, delivering us from the hum drum drum beat into surprise.

Litany as Spiritual Practice and Primordial Reassurance

Formal litany began as a prayer in which the clergy and the congregation acted out call and response.

From the desire of being esteemed, Deliver me, Jesus.
From the desire of being loved, Deliver me, Jesus.
From the desire of being extolled, Deliver me, Jesus.

And so on.

Our longing for both reassurance and surprise led us to adopt religious litany as a poetic form, and this form has become popular universally. We encounter it even in children's books such as *Goodnight Moon:*

Goodnight comb
Goodnight brush
Goodnight nobody
Goodnight mush . . .

Repetition as Primordial Anchor

In Anne Waldman's thirty-page poem "Fast Speaking Woman" she anchors the beginning of each line with a single "I'm" and ends each line with a single "woman."

I'm an abalone woman
I'm the abandoned woman
I'm the woman abashed, the gibberish woman, ...

Her poem is a classic instance of anchoring each line at the left margin with the same, incantatory and reassuring word/sound.

Litany often plays a part in free verse as well. When I was commissioned by Jean Watson at The Center for Human Caring to write *Midwife,* a collection of poems that described caregivers and their work, I wrote a free verse poem in which passages of litany appear.

Skin

Because skin is the first organ
    to form in the womb, and first things
    are of first importance

Because skin is the largest
    organ—an adult's skin weighs six pounds
    and stretched out covers eighteen square feet—

Because the skin's resilience
    can only be experienced

Because it feels superior by far
    to silk or challis

    and in addition is lovely
    to look at, nothing by Cardin
    comes close to it

Because it's the organ with which we experience wind,
    which most loves water,

Because it's the organ through which we begin
    to discover each other

because, because, because, and for all these good reasons

hurry out and touch someone now! Delay
in this matter is not
a good idea, you have delayed too long
already, your suffering brothers and sisters
are waiting, you can hardly expect them to wait
much longer, and remember, when you touch
another person, the skin
gives off a chemical which makes them, and you
    feel better

more alert
more cheerful
more willing to take chances
more open to new experience
more generally obstreperously intend on securing
the greatest good for everybody
and more likely to say NO to the B-1 Lancer bomber
and YES to the levy for the public schools.

After all, it's
the organ

through which we take in
the light we give out

The single word *because* begins the poem so that the hearer may anchor in the comfort of repetition. Then the poem shifts us to the eight-line passage of variation so that we may feel open, free and expansive. Near the finale, there appears again the anchoring, five-line litany of the word *more.* At this point we've experienced a satisfying balance between repetition and variation, and are ready for the closure of the final image: "the light we give out."

Repetition and Variation as Praise

"Saying Things" is a love song I wrote to language. It invites listeners to hear, appreciate and speak single words, each for its own uniqueness.

Three things quickly, pineapple, sparrow grass, whale
and then on to asbestos. What I want to say tonight
is words, the naming of things into their thing,
yucca, brown sugar, solo, the roll of a snare drum,
say something, anything, you'll see what I mean. . . .

The repeating litany is the command "say." And for thirty-five more lines, "say" keeps the base note going, each repetition of that base note balanced by the variant words that follow. Words have been for me vibrant, flying creatures, and this poem pulls me back through time to that ancient epoch when certain animals rose on their hind legs, walked out of the cave's dark and began to speak sounds. Repetitious litany would have been a tool for remembering, and also a way of honing the act of speaking. "Saying Things" is a hymn of praise to the experiment of "inventing" language.

Litany in Free Verse

It's not uncommon to come upon bits of litany in what is essentially a free verse poem. In my example below there are two players: the left and right hands. The left has the potential for cooperation and harmony, and the right for acquisition and destruction.

Poem for the Left and Right Hands

The left hand trails in the water
The right is tying knots

The right stitches a seam
The left sleeps in the silk

The right eats
The left listens under the table

The right swears
The left wears the rings

The right wing, the right loses
The left holds the cards

The left strikes chords while the right
runs, runs, up and down, up and down

and when the right can't sleep and travels
around the world against the clock
the left is buried

Oh left hand, you're so quiet
Do you have children, a dog, mistresses, debts

It's the right that buys the groceries
shifts gears
runs for high office
feeds the baby little silver spoonfuls
It's the right that grabs the knife
to hack off the left hand

The left hand waits
a blind dog

holding in its mouth
the right's glove

The knife falls, clatters
The left hand is the right's

Only chance

In this poem repetition and variation enact comparison. In each couplet the left and right are portrayed as utterly differing, complementary and opposing forces.

We sometimes long for the quiet which occurs when two polarities balance each other. At those times life seems a kind of ease. But eventually one polarity or another asserts itself, and we are lifted into ecstasy or flung down in despair. It's the nature of litany in poetry to play off repetition and variation against each other in a comparative way, and, by that complementary jousting, to arrive at a revealing synthesis.

Litany and Flexibility

The cabinet of poetic forms sets an agreed-upon standard. We decide to adhere to the form and craft a poem. Or we decide to play fast and loose with the form and craft a poem. Of the forms we recognize, litany may well offer the most flexibility. If it appears as a repetitious chant that goes on too long, recognize that this is an opportunity to indulge in a complementary variation. If variation threatens to hold forth too long, bring it back to the home base of repetition. Always allow yourself to adhere to a given pattern in a litany, and always also allow yourself to disobey. Now go out there and play.

IV.

Illustrious Forebears

Marianne Moore's Prose

Antithesis as Modus Operandi

Marianne Moore's *The Complete Prose*, edited by Patricia C. Willis, was published in 1985, thirteen years after Moore's death in 1972—the year when, with MFA in hand, and on the strength of poems published in the *Atlantic*, the *Nation* and the *New Republic*, I began to teach at the University of Colorado in Boulder. Moore's death was a notable event in the poetry world, and I settled in to peruse her history and her oeuvre. Born in Missouri in her Presbyterian grandfather's manse, she'd graduated from Bryn Mawr College, and taught at the Carlisle Indian Industrial School in Carlisle, Pennsylvania, until her first publications in 1915 caught the attention of William Carlos Williams, Wallace Stevens, Pound, Eliot and H.D. From 1925 to 1929, she served as editor of the literary and cultural journal *The Dial*, and her *Collected Poems*, published in 1951, won the Pulitzer, the National Book Award and the Bollingen Prize. Moore had become a colorful celebrity in literary circles. She attended boxing matches and baseball games dressed in a tricorn hat and a black cape, and was a great admirer of Muhammad Ali.

In 1955 Ford Motors petitioned Moore to submit "inspirational names" for their E-car. Her list included "Resilient Bullet," "Ford Silver Sword," "Mongoose Civique," "Varsity Stroke," "Pastelogram," "Andante con Moto" and "Utopian Turtletop"—all a bit arch. Eventually Ford christened the E-car the Edsel, but Moore's panache and her colorful style continued to endear her to the Big Apple scene. She continued in the role of a local celebrity until shortly after throwing the first pitch for the 1968 season in Yankee Stadium, she suffered a stroke. A series of strokes culminated in her death in 1972.

"You won't see anyone as strange as Marianne Moore again," Robert Lowell said, "not for a long while."

Thirteen years later Viking Penguin issued *The Complete Prose of Marianne Moore* in which she quotes Socrates. "I would rather die having spoken in my manner than speak in your manner and live." Moore quotes his statement as an example of antithesis, which she believed was a device writers use instinctively in mastering their subjects. And studying Moore's prose does indeed suggest that Socrates' antithesis was a fundamental fact not just of her writing but of her manner of being.

Lowell's amazed, baffled remark acknowledges the fact that Moore stood out. She lived, as it were, a life of antithesis, in opposition to the norm for a woman of her time: a woman writing, a woman unmarried, and a woman who openly remarked that chastity has "a certain power." The authoritative tone of the prose, like that of the poetry, reveals how determined she was to write her way into the world's attention. Within the confines of her circumstances, she insisted on the absolute accuracy and rightness of her manner of speaking.

The Complete Prose of Marianne Moore, edited by the curator of the Moore Collection at the Rosenbach Museum and Library, is divided into three periods: The Dial Years (1921–1929); The Middle Years (1931–1947); and The Later Years (1948–1968). Appendices include letters to the editor, puffs and short interviews. One gets the feeling that in putting together this collection Willis became so mesmerized by Moore's contradictory indirection that she was demonically inspired not to provide a Table of Contents. The absence of this guide is maddening. Brevity is one of Moore's hallmarks, and the amassing of many very short essays without a retrieval system guarantees Moore fans considerable irritation. One must thumb backward and forward through all six hundred plus pages of text, looking for this piece on Stevens, that review of Bryher.

And how closely the prose resembles the poetry. The stylistic techniques and characteristic manner of thought common to the poems are common to the prose as well. Heavy use of quotation; the despising of connectives; a liking of aphorism; getting at a thing by avoiding the door and coming in through the windows; a predilection for exotic creatures surpassing man—these are her trademarks, always. To a personality like Moore's, the point was precision, and whether she worked in the strophe or the paragraph, her relation to the sentence remained consistently and idiosyncratically hers. Compare:

> Denunciations do not affect
> the culprit: nor blows, but it
> is torture to him not to be spoken to.
> They're natural—
> the coat, like Venus
> mantle lined with stars,
> buttoned close at the neck,—the sleeves new from disuse.

And:

> We are a many-foliaged tree against the moon;
> a wave penetrated by the sun. Some authors
> do not muse within themselves; they "think"
> —like the vegetable shredder which cuts into
> the life of a thing. Miss Bishop is not one
> of these frettingly intensive machines.

In an essay entitled "Feeling and Precision" Moore wrote, "you don't devise a rhythm, the rhythm is the person, and the sentence but a radiograph of personality."

A radiography of personality. How much, in the prose, is left unspoken. Moore had much to say, but more precisely (and I must be precise, I feel she would wish it so), she had much to say on selected subjects, cagily chosen. On other subjects—fascinating—she is mum. This "autobiography," alternately loquacious and silent, provides a tracery of her whimsical, very particularistic reticence, her impulse both to exposit and omit. The omissions pique my curiosity. I like to imagine her gratified and amused by my seeking and my consequent satisfaction and frustration. For her manner of speaking and her decision to address some subjects and avoid others is challenging.

To talk, to be silent. To reveal, and to secrete away. These two complementary psychological impulses manifest themselves in almost every essay, in both style and content. The reader is led from epigram through embellishment and back again to the succinct *mot.* "We are often reminded that the civilized world is uncivilized" is followed by paragraphs of ornate evidence of this claim, punctuated now and again by epigrammatic summary statements, such as "The wish of Mr. Rockefeller that there should be a new museum of antiquities in Egypt seems generous" and (quoting Lewis Carroll) "no deed of ours on this side of the grave is really unselfish." Interplay between capsule and embellishment is characteristic. Her much quoted remarks on Eisenhower in 1961 are a charming illustration from the later work.

> I am deplored for extolling President Eisenhower for the very reasons for which I should reprehend him. Attacked for vetoing the Farm Bill—April 1956—he said, "To produce more crops when we need less, squandering resources on what we cannot eat or sell . . . would it solve the problem? Is it in the best interests of all?" Anything reprehensible in that?

Of Elizabeth Bishop, Moore wrote: "The specific is judiciously interspersed with generality." The same applies to Moore herself. Evidence of Moore's impulse to speak out AND to keep silent is her interest in this phenomenon in others. Moore notes in both Eliot and Stevens that quality she calls "reticent candor." Both, she asserts, achieve "emphasis by understatement." And in a review of H.D.'s *Collected Poems,* Moore tells us they "present a fastidious prodigality—an apparent starkness which is opulence." Oxymoron amounts to an aesthetic, both inscribed and lived.

To reveal, to secrete. Though the majority of the essays address literary matters, the occasional essays are so varied as to suggest an all-inclusiveness—baseball, Abe Lincoln, greed, Churchill, the educating of artists, Brooklyn, fashions in dress, Bryn Mawr, courage, psychoanalysis, "contagion" in poetry, Henry James, humility, the sculpture of Malvina Hoffman.

Yet there are subjects surely of interest to her, which she does not speak to. We learn little, for instance, about Moore's opinion of Modernism as a movement. And yet at least one scholar, Taffy Martin, has made a case for Moore's advance action, describing her not simply as a Modernist but as a writer who anticipated the postmodern as well. What the prose reveals is that Moore appears to be pleased to be included among Modernists; but *her* view of the Modernist aesthetic is almost always purely descriptive. She quotes and reiterates the pronouncements of Eliot, Pound, Stevens and Williams, but makes few pronouncements of her own. Seldom does she qualify her descriptive praise of The Gang of Four, so that instances of even mild rebuke stand out. "Mr. Stevens is never inadvertently crude; one is conscious, however, of a deliberate bearishness—a shadow of acrimonious, unprovoked contumely." It is as though she did not wish to question her hard won but often unacknowledged place in the world of letters.

Her truly severe critique is reserved for Donald Allen's *The New American Poetry: 1945–1960.* She makes clear that her sympathies lie with her generation. Even so, she is at pains to praise individual writers in the anthology and to direct criticism at the group's aesthetic instead. She quarrels with Olson's "Projective Verse," but does not so much criticize it as restate the matter in terms which satisfy her as Olson's do not. With regard to content in general, she asserts:

> Good content, as Samuel Butler said, is usually matched by good treatment, and poets specializing in "organs and feelings"—severed from culture and literature, dogged by redundance and stench—have a stiff task. By comparison with the vocabularies of science, which are creative, in fact enthralling, exhibitionist content—invaded by the diction of drug-vendors and victims, sex addicts and civic parasites—becomes poetically inoperative. "Imagination can be forced," as Alfred Kazin said, "but it cannot be simulated."

Her final pronouncement is that the "essential thing in form is to be free in whatever form is used. A free form does not assure freedom. . . ."

Though she does not directly discuss either literary friendships or literary quarrels of the time, her outspokenness in criticizing *The New American Poetry* (*The,* she thought, should be omitted from the title) suggests she might have liked to but felt constrained. A pity, for she might have done so charmingly, given her wit, her perspicacity, her bright eye and her sharp though bridled tongue. An essay in *The Dial* in December 1926 comes as close as Moore came to articulating her view of the relation of contemporary artists to one another. The essay asserts, among other things, that in "blindly disparaging another, one shows merely that one envies him his realness and wishes that he were what one says he is." Moore subsumes the contradictions that must have arisen between her contemporaries, and between herself and them, into the syntheses she probably wished. Although "the judgment of experts on one another is at variance," she writes, "their genius is not; perception is always, as Traherne would say, 'innocent.'"

Similarly, Moore says little about the status of women writers in her own time or in previous periods. I imagine she would have considered "rising above" gossip to be a virtue, but even so, she does not address either women writers or women as a group, nor does she interrogate their circumstances. She quotes Confucius. "What you don't want, don't inflict on others." She also said, "There is nothing I dislike more than the exposé or any kind of revenge." On the other hand she could be gabby about Henry James or the Cantos. And when she does speak, it's with absolute authority and the certainty that the world agrees with her. *We*, she says, asserting her accord with society at large.

Why not then spout her own view of matters aesthetic? Why not discuss the position of women, both in and out of the literary world? Given her penchant for being on the side of virtue, wouldn't such matter be her meat? Helen Vendler, in her essay on Moore in the *Modern Critical Views* series, suggests that Moore was simply too exotic for America. Since Moore values understatement, Vendler suggests that it may have seemed to Moore "that most people around her were shouting, and that buried or dry phrases from her would be 'mute' to them. It may be that she gave up hope . . . of reaching a general audience. . . ."

There is surely truth in Vendler's supposition, but at the same time it would seem that a woman of Moore's intelligence would have known the score only too well. As Suzanne Juhasz writes in *Naked and Fiery Forms*, "Marianne Moore did not exaggerate her sense of danger. In her life and in her art she trod delicately, purposefully, skillfully through enemy lines, deflecting attack by eluding it, by denying it, by never appearing to be at battle. . . ." With the exception of the poem "Marriage," Moore does not directly address relations between the sexes at all. And her rare remarks about women are contradictory. She speaks at length of Carey Thomas' tribulations, describing Thomas as "sobered by obstruction." Thomas, Moore writes, the "virtual administrator and dean of a college, was made president officially by a majority of but one vote; then only after years of 'wary foresight in holding back and driving forward at the right moments,' was grudgingly elected to the board of trustees." Yet in the next breath Moore asserts that "women are no longer debarred from the professions that are open to men," as though the matter had since been settled once and for all.

What Marianne Moore did do was to review books by women writers with care and considerable enthusiasm. Her reviews of H.D., Bryher and Bogan are fully as admiring as those of Auden, Williams, Stevens, Pound and Cummings. She describes H.D. as one in whom we find "intensive, unmixed and unimpeded, the white fire of the poet." With wit and acerbity she defends Dickinson against accusations of vanity.

> A certain buoyancy that creates an effect of inconsequential bravado—a sense of drama with which we may not be quite at home—was for her part of that expansion of breath necessary to existence, and unless it is conceited for the hummingbird or the osprey to not behave like a chicken, one does not find her conceited.

And in reply to Dame Edith's father's remark that "Edith will commit suicide when she finds she cannot write poetry," Moore writes dryly that "need for this has not arisen." Though Moore did not review Amy Lowell's work, she wrote *The Dial*'s eulogy, describing Lowell as a "self-dependently American, sometimes modern American writer."

> The death of Amy Lowell emphasizes the force of her personality. Cosmopolitan yet isolated, essentially distinct from "the imagist group" of which she has been called "the recognized

spokesman," she has by a misleadingly armored self-reliance, sometimes obscured a generosity, a love of romance, and the luster of a chivalry which was essentially hers.

Moore could be cutting, but her infrequent sharp remarks are generally reserved for her male contemporaries. A one-sentence review of *Chills and Fever*, by John Crowe Ransom, reads:

> Unrewarding dissonances, mountebank persiflage, mock medieval minstrelsy, and shreds of elegance disturbingly suggestive of now this, now that contemporary bard, deprive one of the faculty to diagnose this "dangerous" phenomenon to which one has exposed oneself.

In her review of *The New American Poetry,* she manages to compliment Allen Ginsberg, then adds by the by, that he "can foul the nest in a way to marvel at."

Though it appears Moore made a conscious decision to be unfailingly gracious toward her female contemporaries, her praise is occasionally couched in attitudes we would now describe as male-biased. It is today a left-handed compliment to say, as Moore does of Bogan, that one is struck by her "restraint," that "women are not noted for terseness, but Louise Bogan's art is compactness compacted." Such praise too closely resembles Auden's treatment of Adrienne Rich's early poems, which he wrote were "neatly and modestly dressed, speak quietly but do not mumble, respect their elders but are not cowed by them, and do not tell fibs."

Moore will not decide to speak to woman's condition generally, but when questioned on this matter for the *Encyclopedia Year Book* (1957), she responds:

> With regard to careers outside the home, delegated motherhood can be a threat, for I believe that our integrity as a nation is bound up with the home. Good children are not the product of mothers who prefer money or fame to the well-being of their families. . . . We dare not regress by suppressing intelligence or forbidding women to be useful. But steadfastness, conscience and the capacity for sacrifice . . . are basic . . .

Such a statement gives us pause. Then we remember Moore's context. She died before Mary Daly had reclaimed the word *spinster,* thus accomplishing what Moore most devoutly wished and heartily approved: the passing on of language, as Eliot wrote, "more highly developed, more refined, more precise than it was before."

Moore's "reticent candor," her "fastidious prodigality," are a challenge. Precision is not clarity, nor is it autobiography. What, were it known, might have been the true state of affairs? Recent feminist criticism acknowledges, from a range of perspectives, Moore's sometimes obvious, often hidden, power. In *Naked and Fiery Forms,* Suzanne Juhasz makes the case that Moore did not escape the double bind of the woman writer, and remarks Moore's "marked exclusion of feminine experience from art." Still Juhasz notes that Moore's separation in herself of woman and poet gained her "a victory that may have been qualified by the very methods used to gain it but which was nevertheless a prize that few before her had won." In *Marianne Moore: The Poet's Advance,* Laurence Stapleton reads "Granite and Steel" as a corrective to Hart Crane's "grandiose vision of a voyage to Atlantis" and as affirmation of the mind's power. Vendler does not see Moore's "armored" stance as defensive but as one of "superior amusement and denigration." She reads "Black Earth" as a description of the self in much the same way Alicia Ostriker, in *Stealing the Language,* sees "Sojourn in the Whale" as a portrait of relations between the sexes. Vendler also points out that male critics of Moore make her out to be "more shrinking and squeamish than she is."

> There is no doubt something in Moore that elicits this uneasiness in male commentators, no matter how strongly they extol her virtues. Perhaps her work is in fact more "feminine" than it may appear. . . . Or perhaps Moore's occasional contempt for the world of male power provokes a counterattack on what may seem to some her miniature version of life.

In *Marianne Moore: Subversive Modernist,* Taffy Martin refuses the view that Moore's proper place is within the European mode of Modernism, where her craft and precision are perceived as "defensive barriers around her." Martin makes the case that Moore was thoroughly in Williams' American stream, and that she acted as a subversive influence within it. Discussing Moore's years at *The Dial,* Martin points out that during Thayer's editing of the magazine, he attempted to build it into a bulwark against the contradictions of the age, and that once Moore became editor, she turned *The Dial* into an "aesthetic equivalent" of those contradictions. She "was as opinionated and determined as she was retiring and private," Martin states, and she altered *The Dial*'s previously defensive tone and "conducted" as one does an orchestra, by

> enacting in her essays the multiplicity and disparateness of the world around her. Moore's essays present judgments, just as Thayer's do, but they are positive judgments that accept and mirror rather than attempt to diminish the fragmentation of the modern world.

Thus for Martin, Moore represents "a playful rather than a defensive spirit."

Playfulness thrives on secrecy, indirection, sleight of hand. Now you see her, now you don't. This, this, and this, but not that, my friends. The prose most certainly enacts Williams' "necessary appearance of disorder in all immediacy," but it also serves as a screen from behind which Moore steps fleetingly, unpredictably. "The unquiet nature of the artist is proverbial, genius being in some sense always in revolt," she says, apparently speaking of someone other than herself. But is she? Responding to questions put to her by Howard Nemerov, she remarks, "I see no revolution in 'the artist.'" Here she seems to speak for herself. But again, does she?

"It is typical of Miss Moore's poetry that the meaning is equivocal," Donald Hall said. "She gives and takes away with the same motion, so that often, just as one believes he understands, the words start to fold back on themselves and an exactly opposite meaning begins to seem plausible." Hall's statement reminds us of Freud's belief that contradiction is a fact of the unconscious. Dreams often combine and accommodate contrary things, and in the unconscious, contradictory thoughts exist side by side.

In "Feeling and Precision" Moore makes an intriguing assertion. "Instinctively, we employ antithesis as an aid to precision. . . ." She is speaking of writing, but she might as well have spoken for herself. Here, and in countless other assertions, she proclaims her authority, proceeding as though she and the world agree, when in fact she lived a life in contrast to quotidian expectations. *We,* she says, asserting publicly her accord with a milieu which perceived her as "strange." "Instinctively, we"—but since we all do not instinctively act as she asserts, the emphasis is thrown onto the adverb. And the adverb suggests the personal. It is as though she had in fact said, "Instinctively, I."

Antithesis.

Reticent candor.

Moore, the oxymoron.

In 1962 *Esquire* asked Moore to state her "most paradoxical quality." Her reply: "Like to be inconspicuous but look well." Perhaps her penchant for perceiving oxymoron and her talent for being one are her attempt to achieve balance, the Greeks' moderation which she so often professed to admire. In H.D., Moore found "the verbal continuity, the controlled ardor, the balanced speech of poetry." She consistently criticized extremes. "Egotism is usually subversive of sagacity," she declared. ". . . excess is the common substitute for energy." And in *The Complete Prose* Moore twice quotes Confucius: "If there be a knife of resentment in the heart, the mind fails to attain precision."

She may have hoped for balance, but it is an existential fact that its achievement is never permanent. Pushed too far, one is likely to declare the bottom line. *I would rather die having spoken in my manner than speak in your manner and live.* Socrates' declaration leaps from Moore's page, a *cri de coeur.* "Originals are better than replicas," she wrote, and stands as an illustration of her assertion.

Akhmatova

The Leper's Rattle

> It's not with a lover's lyre, not at all,
> That I go around attracting a crowd.
> It's the rattle with which lepers crawl
> That in my hands keeps singing aloud.
> —Anna Akhmatova
> *(translated by Lyn Coffin)*

The poem: for all the reasons it's wrong it's right. It lacks, happily, the preciousness of the minimal. This poem is not a gem, but resembles instead a stick of dynamite—small package, whopping effect.

It's a chestnut, yes, didactic in intent, its program oversimplified—except for its reverberations. From what appears to be simple—diction, form, statement—springs an elaborate discernment. The poem goes after the speaker's detractors with a finely tuned spirit of revenge. Akhmatova aimed for truth, and truth is its own naked force. "I don't understand these big words," she once said, "poet, billiard."

It's got the mindless, singsong personality of a nursery rhyme, tossed off. Tossed off for the sake of the rhyme, that indulgence which defeats subtlety—except that this poem travels powered by such rhyme. And who can ignore the passing of a diesel truck?

But isn't it histrionic, for her, a mature writer? As the generation of our parents might say, "At her age!" Except that just such an unexpected turn, of just that intensity, is characteristic of Akhmatova. Passion, after all, was her way of life. "An element of howl," as Joseph Brodsky has pointed out, is one of her hallmarks. So we admire the poem's blatancy. The take it or leave it tone. The way it goes about its business slamming doors, breaking china, shattering crystal against the hearth. How it mocks subtlety. Daring to speak as she feels at that moment, unguarded and utterly frank, flatfooted, bald, short to the point almost of crudity but right on target—to such daring how we're drawn.

And then the whack of the imagery. What nerve in a woman, writing, to set the lover square against the leper in the poem. It suggests the easy dualism of stereotype: virgin/whore, princess/monster. Except that Akhmatova does this on purpose, to fling the dualism in our faces. She insists that we understand just how crude such oppositions are, how they mask reality. We respond to the audacity with which she seems to say, "They want good girls? Then I'll be bad." And its counterpart: "They want bad girls? Then I'll be BAD!"

The poem takes a quantum leap when we know that the diction is literally autobiographical. It is true that Akhmatova's first books spoke the *lingua franca* of romantic love. What is also true is that critics' insistence that her significance was as a writer of love lyrics was part of the move to silence her politically, humanly. These pronouncements mirrored the state's censorship of her work between 1923 and 1940. Precisely because she did *not* restrict her work to the production of the obligatory and harmless, she suffered. Her first husband, Gumiliov, was executed, probably on direct order from Lenin. Her close friend Mandelstam died in a concentration camp. Her son Lev was imprisoned, and her third husband Punin died in prison. About these sorrows and the sorrow she felt for her country under Stalin's thumb she was forbidden to speak, and her work was banned. Thus she became, as the poem states so flatly, a leper. In the state's official view she was *persona non grata.*

But the poem describes her triumph as an untouchable. It is when the speaker is most dangerous, when she is most infectious, that she draws crowds. Just so Akhmatova spoke for and thus drew to her all those who, like her, suffered at the hands of the state, that suffering comprising nearly all Russians. Thus a leprous speaker becomes a spiritual leader. These lines are spoken by a charismatic voice. And it is the charisma of the survivor who not only survives but triumphs.

It is also the charisma of the survivor who lifts an awful truth up from darkness. Love is and lovers are blind, remember. But lepers see, and what she sees is what the crowd also sees: that the Emperor has no clothes. Thus the poem rings out across cultures and down through our present epoch. Akhmatova was and we are citizen residents of opposing "superpowers" which, in that superiority only brute power can confer, have come to resemble each other.

All of us here who dissent are made to feel we go not just against the Reagan era but against the American grain. Just so Akhmatova was proclaimed traitorous not to Stalin (she was forced to sing his praises in order to secure her son's release from prison) but to the ideals of the Russian nation. And yet in the poem, in the speaker's hands, the rattle sings aloud. The poem does what only the single quatrain can do so well. It falls progressively downward through the first three lines, then soars into and beyond the final line, astonishing us. Think for instance of Dickinson's version of that stanza:

> Because I could not stop for Death—
> He kindly stopped for me—
> The Carriage held but just Ourselves—
> And Immortality.

Because the third line of Akhmatova's poem ends with the image of the leper crawling—ends with the word *crawl,* that leprous word—and how much lower can we fall than to *crawl*—the final line's lifting-off feels like an immense surge.

The imagery too ("that rattle with which lepers crawl") has the intensity of nursery rhyme. Think how, in the lines "ashes, ashes, / we all fall down" the word *ashes* resonates to our ear. That verse recreates the atmosphere of the Middle Ages and the Plague, which made everyone "fall down," the infection which required that the bodies be burned: ashes. Similarly, in Akhmatova's poem, the lyre is too delicate an instrument with which to capture the true character of her century.

We live still in a time of war, of epidemic, of famine amidst plenty, of the wasting of the earth. Ours is a time of blunt events, reeling reactions, a time of fear and cowering. Of crawling. As Joseph Brodsky writes in the introduction to Lyn Coffin's selection and translation of Akhmatova, the poet's work, characterized by "the note of controlled terror," took Russian poetry into "the real, non-calendar twentieth century."

Not the lyre but the rattle. Its drama, its repetitive insistence, its foreboding whirr, like the sound of a rattlesnake's tail striking that note of controlled terror—the rattle is the proper instrument of our epoch. How fitting then that the rattle, monochromatic, is an instrument of one tone only. It conveys no melody. Rhythm is its business. It can only mark time. And yet in Akhmatova's hands, the music of lyric poetry is neither lost nor blunted. For her, the rattle "keeps singing aloud."

W. S. Merwin's "One Story"

A Tribute

Always somewhere in the story
which up until now we thought
was ours whoever it was
that we were being then
had to wander out into
the green towering forest
reaching to the end of
the world and beyond older
than anything whoever
we were being could remember
and find there that it was
no different from the story
anywhere in the forest
and never be able to tell
as long as the story was there
whether the fiery voices
now far ahead now under
foot the eyes staring from
their instant that held the story
as one breath the shadows
offering their spread flowers
and the chill that leapt from its own
turn through the hair of the nape
like a light through a forest
knew the untold story
all along and were waiting
at the right place as the moment
arrived for whoever it was
to be led at last by the wiles
of ignorance through the forest

and come before them face
to face for the first time
recognizing them with
no names and again surviving
seizing something alive
to take home out of the story
but what came out of the forest
was all part of the story
whatever died on the way
or was named but no longer
recognizable even
what vanished out of the story
finally day after day
was becoming the story
so that when there is no more
story that will be our
story when there is no
forest that will be our forest

Our losses once seemed provisional. There were and would be other actors, and thus other losses. No loss was final. There was always more to lose. But "One Story" reminds us that we live in a time of vanishing. In *A Flight of Swans* Tagore wrote:

Life is now drunk with the sport of death—
Welcome Him with all that you have.
Look neither to the right nor left,
Keep nothing hidden,
And touch His feet with your forehead—
Now the All-Destroying is come.

We know the story is not ours. We are in it, but it doesn't belong to us. Instead we belong to it. We are belongings held in the Great Belonging.

What can Belongings do? There was a time on this planet when there was only a tiny bit of oxygen in the atmosphere. Then, gradually, one thing led to another, and a lot more oxygen came on the scene. So the blue-green bacteria took up the challenge. It's beginning to sound like Hollywood, isn't it. The blue-green bacteria created a way to live with what was killing them. They brought on the Oxygen Revolution in which they created oxygen photosynthesis. They turned themselves into oxygen breathers and became the progenitors of mitochondria, those movie stars of the nucleated cell.

This is a plot: triumph over adversity.

Hollywood will make the movie.

Hollywood won't make the movie of "One Story."

Because vanishing is not a plot.

So: what do belongings do? You are alive, you see what is really there, and you take destruction inside you and transform it. It comes out of you as creation. You put something beautiful and true back into the world.

The beautiful thing is the poem. I receive "One Story" as the gift it is. Lewis Hyde points out that the gift stays alive as long as it keeps moving. Thus I receive it, and by calling your attention to it now, move it on. Obviously this is not an occasion of scholarship or of business. I write of the gift as a way of honoring poem and giver. In this stance, a kind of kneeling, poem and giver are before me, and I am blessed and humbled.

Merwin is a poet who understands that the poems he "writes" are gifts given by the natural landscape around him. He is a poet who sits, waits and receives, and writes this down.

> In Zen there is the practice of just sitting.
> We don't want to accomplish anything.
> We are present, and attentive—
> and the door is ajar.

V.

Poetry as a Way of Witnessing

The Poetry of Witness

Then, and Now

In 1960 when John Kennedy was elected President, I was a freshman. I'd read all of Faulkner's novels in my senior year of high school to keep from going crazy. Now Kennedy spoke as though directly to me. Our world, he said, was filled with "tyranny, poverty, disease, and war itself." Thus our work as citizens would not be finished in the first hundred days, nor even in our lifetime. "But let us begin," he said.

I was studying French, and planned to travel to Paris the following summer. But no one in Paris needed me, whereas my President urged me to succor those in the far-flung hinterlands of tyranny, poverty, disease, war. I'd read Auden's *September 1, 1939,* but I'd not heard the term "poetry of witness." It was some years later, in 1976, that Carolyn Forché's *Gathering the Tribes* won the Yale Series of Younger Poets Competition. She then went to El Salvador to work as a human rights advocate, and began collecting poems for her groundbreaking anthology *Against Forgetting: Twentieth-Century Poetry of Witness.*

Though the Sixties, Seventies and Eighties, American poets witnessed Civil Rights strife, the Vietnam war protests, the Kent state murders, the murder of the Kennedy brothers and King. Distinction between personal and political disappeared. Nobel poet Wisława Szymborska wrote:

> Whether you like it or not
> Your genes have a political past,
> Your skin a political cast,
> Your eyes a political slant.
> Whatever you say reverberates,

whatever you don't say speaks for itself.
So either way you're talking politics.

Some American poets witnessed atrocities of gender, race and class in their own country. Others began to witness abroad. Forché offered the image of the colonel spilling his grocery bag of human ears onto the dining room table, an image that remains unforgettable. We will remember her for establishing testimonial art as a genre.

My first poem of witness was a double sestina, composed in 1980, exploring the contrast between Emma Goldman's and Alexandra Kollontai's polar strategies as females in a male political milieu. Kollontai was Lenin's Chairwoman of the Ministry for Social Welfare. The statement that in Communist societies the satisfaction of sexual desires will be as unremarkable as drinking a glass of water was wrongly attributed to her. Though several of her lovers died in Stalinist purges, her forty-eight-page memoir reveals little of the trepidation and anguish she fielded under Lenin. In contrast Goldman was a confident, colorful revolutionary who loved opera and was known for buying herself roses. When her lover objected on grounds that their funds should be spent on bread for the hungry, she insisted that beauty was an important "bread."

Examining these contrasting figures was preparation for witnessing. Writers walk a spiritual path that engages heart, mind, soul, and ours is a political *and* a spiritual labor. We who work at universities enjoy the safety of the cloister, but the cloister may also constrict the artist.

You must change your life, Rilke wrote. So in 1992 I took a semester's leave from teaching to work in Sri Lanka for Peace Brigade International. Around the planet the verb "disappear" had morphed into a terrifying noun: "the disappeared." And as war between the Sinhalese majority and the Tamil minority escalated and government death squads proliferated, human rights advocates faced their government's death squads. When the Bar Association had lost five lawyers to death squad murders, they invited PBI to open a project on the island. PBI's leverage depended on the fact that if the government wanted foreign aid, it must treat donor countries' citizens with respect.

I had not come to South Asia to gather "material" for writing. But I met Sri Lankans from every level of society eager to describe losing family members, voicing fear that they might become targets too. Tell Americans, they said. Americans will help us.

The Sinhalese army's most flagrant atrocity was a massacre near the Tamil village of Kokodicholai. Some Sinhalese government soldiers were killed by a land mine, and in the next day's retaliation, their buddies raped and murdered over a hundred villagers. One witness watched the soldiers herd village men into the land mine's crater.

After the mine the soldiers came
Among those men they took was my husband
They made the men circle the crater three times
Then the soldiers forced them into the center

The third one herded in was my husband
Where I hid I could see his face as they shot him
I watched as one by one the others fell
Their bodies one above the other, sticks of wood

I have seven children I know my husband's body
After the burning I did not know his body
After the burning I did not see his face again
The cloth is a piece of his sarong, partly burned

I recorded the stories of those who'd witnessed atrocities. And I accompanied a physician midwife, Dr. Saravannamuttu. Her son, a respected reporter, had been murdered by a death squad, and she had helped form the Mothers' Front.

Because when they came for her son she saw their faces,
I walked into the dirt street with this woman
they wanted to kill. We knew they were watching,
they could shoot her and leave me alive, or shoot us both—

either would prove they could kill anyone they wanted—
and they needed that fleeting bit of power, they had

so little. . . .

Sri Lankans offered me spontaneous tenderness, securing a seat for me on a crowded bus, offering me water in fiery, equatorial heat, and I'd acted in good faith as a mirror of their fear.

Evening, a child cries,
A woman stirs something in a pot
Because when they've carried away the dead
Those who are left will want to eat. When dark

Comes and you're alive, you want to kiss
The beggar at the gate, the crippled clerk,
Even the general who knew about the disappearances
And let them go on. . . .

"To acquire a political meaning," Szymborska writes,

you don't even have to be human.
Raw material will do,
or protein feed, or crude oil,

or a conference table whose shape
was quarreled over for months:
Should we arbitrate life and death
At a round table or a square one.

"Meanwhile," she continues, "people perished. . . ."

In the anguish I felt for Sri Lankans, I began a poem composed of numbered sequences. Each sequence, composed of couplets, zeroed in on an atrocity here, an interior monologue there, in my country and abroad. The poem moved backward and forward in time and place, building a mosaic of physical, psychological atrocities. It began with a scene in a jungle:

Look: see the peasant blasted at his crop.
The refugees kidnapped, made to carry ammunition.

The missiles dismantled, rebuilt, reinstalled.
The carcinogenic apples, the bereft gorilla mother. . . .

Through the first twelve sections the poem's darkness and contraction increased and filled with *confutatus* and *lacrimoso.* Section 12 portrayed Hedda Nussbaum, the battered woman whose face appeared on the cover of *Time* magazine, and who, with her lover, may have assisted in her daughter's murder.

Black is the color of my true love's hair
Black is the color of her face, its torn flap. . . .

Black is the color of the first day I let him hurt her
Black is the color of the first day I helped him hurt her. . . .

I wanted to address not just Asian violence but American violence as well. And now the poem had hit bottom. I understood then that just as Mozart's Requiem turns from anguish and begins to rise, my requiem too would turn and rise—because it must, because we must.

. . . No guard, no torturer, no bureaucrat, no minister,
no gang of toughs, no burglar, no mugger,

no squads, no platoons, no rifles, no bayonets,
no heads on poles, no breasts in piles,

no young ones in ditches burned with gasoline.
No hillsides of skeletons. No pits bulldozed over.

The voice in the *Agnus Dei* and at the Requiem's end is a female voice.

You don't see her? Switch off the instrument panel.
Put down the knife. Don't put food in death's mouth.

Open your hand: the fist disappears. . . .

I'd explored the hell of contraction and the heaven of expansion. We experience these two states which eventually merge and disappear into each other—leaving a unity in which we feel ourselves free, full and whole.

In the second decade of our twenty-first century, as financial markets crash, political corruption flourishes and first world governments wage wars in the third world, poets go on witnessing. To feel a protectiveness toward the world is human. Now that the internet connects us in cyberspace, we see the Egyptian "blue bra" woman being beaten, and we click, and the next day thousands of Egyptian women march in the streets shouting, being heard.

Clicking works to organize millions, but poets must do more than respond online. We must write from our cloisters, then leave our cloisters, and stand beneath sky and shout solidarity with Tunisian fruit and vegetable vendor Mohamed Bouazizi who will set himself on fire; with the Mexican illegal in L.A. working for less than minimum wage; with Gaza journalist Vittorio Arrigoni, and the homeless woman charged with larceny for giving a false address to keep her child in school. As Bertolt Brecht said:

> In dark times will there be singing?
> Yes, there will be singing.
> About the dark times.

Peripatetic Witnesses

Karen Swenson and Mary Crow

A woman student, gang-raped in India, dies; in Rio on a public bus a man holds a gun to the head of a young woman and rapes her in front of the passengers; in a Rio transit van men gang-rape a visiting American student, pummeling her face, beating her companion with a steel bar. And in the U.S. rapes in the armed forces continue. Indecencies—atrocities—go on. There are the frightened and the angry and those who don't want to know in detail the human failure to live "humanely."

Meanwhile others like the poet Karen Swenson serve as witnesses by working with PEN America to free prisoners of conscience and also enact private spiritual pilgrimage. Swenson is a graduate of Barnard College and New York University. Her books include *A Daughter's Latitude* (Copper Canyon Press, 1999); *The Landlady in Bangkok* (1993), which was selected for the National Poetry Series; *A Sense of Direction* (1989); *An Attic of Ideals* (1974); and the chapbook *East-West* (1980). As citizens we're automatically deputized as witnesses simply by appearing where a violent act is in progress. Ironic then that in the first section of her latest collection of poetry, *A Pilgrim Into Silence,* Swenson witnesses her own human failings.

In "Thanksgiving" she looks back and re-inhabits the pain of her younger self with compassionate insight. Her son knew her

> not as slaps and yells, but the mother, muffled in
> a stale swaddle of beer, who appearing present,
> was untouchable, a figment of the bottle's
> imagination.

I salute Swenson, for I have been there too, living my own ambivalence. Though I had the best intentions, I was myopic. My child signaled her distress, and I knew and saw and yet could not find ways to address her unspoken but visible need. Similarly, in another poem, experience primes Swenson to recognize herself at the opera as "an unaccompanied decomposition / conducted by gin through scene after scene."

The subsequent three sections of this collection address Swenson's spiritual pilgrimages abroad. "Tashi, 1936–2002" is a harrowing account of China's Cultural Revolution and its takeover of Tibet. The poem's first line: "The cadre yanks the pearls from her neck, smiles." Later Tashi is imprisoned in "a knitting factory, ten women shut in a room, / their wailing children, shut out, eat gutter scraps. . . ." Tashi's husband is sentenced to starvation, hoeing "potatoes, eyes sharp for / a gulp of worm, a lizard feast." He eats the lizard and receives a beating. In rendering these scorching scenes, Swenson is careful not to inflate her rhetoric.

At Mother Teresa's hospice in Calcutta, Swenson declines pity for the suffering, instead admiring their persevering against formidable odds. She conveys her respect

> for the sheer willfulness of life—a blind
> and cornered cat slashing at Death's dogs.

In "The Chicago Hermit at Mother Teresa's," Swenson describes a young volunteer as

> a slim young heron, raw
> at ankle and red wrist-bone,
> earnest and Irish, ashamed
> of his body. That traitor's become
> a sinister foreigner with
> an anarchist penis, an umbrella
> in a wind storm, leading him
> to no brave new world but a land
> of flesh, where one false move
> will detonate him straight to hell.
> His mouth full of cookies, he sits
> unsmiling over his tea.

I try to draw him out, ask
Are you ill? He shrinks,
a salted snail, at the word
diarrhea and shifts me quickly
to the spirit, says people here,
just ordinary people
have a better grasp of the soul
than his family priest in Chicago.
I enumerate the symptoms
of giardia—diarrhea, cramps, gas—suggest
he go to a clinic but don't explain
that Hindus disbelieve in the soul
and have another cookie.

Swenson withholds judgment, offers compassion. And this stance continues when she returns to the West. "Street Scene" is set on 54th Street in New York. A young woman walking past Swenson (think pilgrimage) begins to weep.

Eyes averted, I pass, see beyond her his straight
back, a furled umbrella cased in a suit without a sigh.
But I must not judge. Perhaps he's had an escape
from need or greed or a mind sweet and silly as Jell-O.
It was just the collapse, the suddenness of her sorrow.

We long to experience transcendence, and to satisfy that longing, Swenson goes on annual pilgrimage to Mount Kailash, which, in Buddhism, is considered the navel of the world. The pilgrimage begins at 15,000 feet, and thirty-three miles later ends at a 18,600-foot pass. In "Circumambulating Mount Kailash" pilgrims come upon remains of a corpse laid out on stone

. . . beneath a long sheep-coat's gray curls.
A man and woman stand beside
this still heap where the wind unfurls
a flag of dust. She's teary-eyed.
He's baffled, as if the hand he
grasped had gone empty as a glove.
The nomads and I on the scree
path pause in homage while we shove
hands into pockets of our packs.

> We've been transformed to Magi whose
> gifts, yak cheese, candy, tsampa, stack
> of silvery coins are tumbling loose
> where death lies swaddled in its stone
> bound manger, . . .

For Swenson, to go on pilgrimage also includes experiencing humility in regard to her disintegrating body. "Always I've thought it would / be like this," she writes, referring to aging's transformation. What any of us have is the present's momentary, fleeting gestalt: ". . . naked rock sharp under sun, / wind singing, sprung steel of a rapier / in my ears."

Poet and translator Mary Crow served as Poet Laureate of Colorado from 1996 to 2010 and has written five collections of poetry. In the Sixties, she sought out Latin American women poets, but lamented finding "only a few names, a few poems." Later her anthology, *Woman Who Has Sprouted Wings: Poems by Contemporary Latin American Women Poets,* garnered Columbia University's Translation Center Award, and she received Fulbright research awards to Chile, Peru, Argentina, Venezuela and Yugoslavia. Her translations include *Vertical Poetry: Last Poems by Roberto Juarroz, Engravings Torn from Insomnia: Poems by Olga Orozco, Vertical Poetry: Recent Poems by Roberto Juarroz,* and *From the Country of Nevermore: Poems by Jorge Teillier.*

Her 1996 collection, *I Have Tasted the Apple,* follows upon the harrowing poems in *Borders.* In his introduction to *Borders,* David Ignatow wrote,

> by the grace and power of her art, the poems . . . are kept from vanishing into the pain itself, thereby making a voice and presence . . . that is the fulfillment of her search for self.

This same artistry powers the poems in *I Have Tasted the Apple.* Sensuousness carries on its poignant argument with anguish. The epigraph from Teillier announces the book's twin themes with this image: "an apple too beautiful to eat right away." In a poem entitled "As If" she proclaims her kinship with the bear "clan." Crow elaborates, so that we understand the dubious context her sensuous identity must mediate. Her Egypt is not Flaubert's. He declared he liked "a touch of bitterness in things," but for Crow, pursued by a stalker, then assaulted on a bus, bitterness has quite a different flavor.

Sensuousness and pain continue their dialectical argument in "Past History," a poem in which a teacher announced that "surrender was feminine, and the missionary / position best." And in "A Mother's Insomnia" Crow renders with chilling vividness the culture of war which will turn her sons into "faces, blank," and spread "over them a calm like the wind's aftermath when only the smell remains."

In the collection's second section she encounters masked students with broken Coke bottles in Venezuela, the Nazi legacy in Poland, a woman's face "beaten shapeless." Poem after poem hammers out its litany of inhumanity. In the third section "Breakdancing" and "Shadows" body forth what Yusef Komunyakaa on the jacket calls "a quiet, honed rage." She describes the "calm that is dead, not peaceful" reigning across much of our postmodern world.

In "Shadows" residents of Sarajevo watch "Dynasty and Dallas as the call for prayer / sails out into the evening air." Crow writes that "the TV / sucks them in as if to take their lives / inside the box," and they must "look around to see . . . who is envying them this blonde. . . ." And Part IV re-invokes Crow's sense of herself as surrounded by suffering. She persists by affirming "the blur, the smear, the blear, / the whole sensual conglomeration of the world."

The final poem, "Swimming," tracks this lyrical self-consciousness through moments of transcendence. Walking through a grove of aspen, Crow experiences the sheer aliveness of nature, and herself one jewel in Indra's Net. This poem closes the collection on a note of transcendent suspension which characterizes the book as a whole: Kurd guerillas appear, and so does the blue jay. Beauty and pain vibrate together, moving on waves of expansion and contraction, as Crow "swims" through air, "into, out of / light? Toward."

Mary Crow's is a large intelligence, welcoming experience with a wide, generous range of response. It's intelligence that doesn't forget that where there's "the blue lake / where the wild horses / come to drink" there is also the destructively exclusive politics of "prayer in the schools." ("It's always Christian, isn't it?") Better than any other contemporary poet I can think of, she renders feeling's diminishment by fear.

> How the animal shuts down,
> cowering on the trail,
> body hunched and flattened.
>
> And the soul folding smaller and smaller,
> trying to hide, to become
> rock or river. ("Escape")

This is a compassionate intelligence that can say, "I don't mind that aging softens everything. / Hold out your hand."

Helen Vendler has remarked in *Soul Says* that there is a moral strenuousness in American poetry. But it's not moral strenuousness that characterizes a Mary Crow poem. It's dismay and a spontaneous, encompassing sorrow. Numbed by market materialism we may avoid reports of rapes and massacres beyond our borders, but Crow faces into the suffering of others and mourns. Hers is a witness deepened by the transforming flame of poetry and female ardor.

The Mythic Dimension of Witness

Berdeshevsky

Margo Berdeshevsky's book of illustrated stories, *Beautiful Soon Enough* (2009) received the American Book Review/Ronald Sukenick Award for Innovative Fiction. Her first collection of poetry, *But A Passage In Wilderness* (2007), was selected by Marie Ponsot for the Poetry Society of America's Robert H. Winner Award, and *Between Soul and Stone* appeared in 2011. Over and over, poem after poem evokes our earthy world, which is at the same time an earthy world rich with spirit and subsumed by spirit. It's Berdeshevsky's intention to act as a sibyl, pointing to these two realms which are one realm, declaring that there can be no earthy world *without* spirit.

In the poem "On Frailty" in *But A Passage In Wilderness* Berdeshevsky establishes femaleness as the ground of her speech. "Let the protector of truth come," she writes, "down from her mythic hill, battered cloche and staff to / pierce the ground so swollen with story." Her poems constantly negotiate a perceived dichotomy between elusive spirit and apparent earth. But the female descending to earth and then ascending toward the spirit realm, back and forth, isn't a mythic allusion used in the cause of self-aggrandizement. She merely renders the world "as it is," pointing to its completeness, showing us, teaching us.

She is the female Sybil, modeling the unity earth/spirit, then rising up as rescuer and protector, and going toward crisis. After the tsunami in Aceh, Sumatra, Berdeshevsky volunteered, reclaiming bodies from the sea, and taking on the tasks of caring for survivors. In *Between Soul and Stone* the poem "Beachfront" she renders again the tsunami's reverberating details. "A wise man of / a village, with so few to be wise for any longer." And this: "There were children hung in trees in a mother's / sarong to be safe. Motherless, safe and staring. . . ."

"Best Love and Goodbye," a ten-page work which laments the phenomenon of war, highlights her voice, blending it with others in the "collage" featuring Camus, Wilfred Owen, Rupert Brooke, Graves and (at last, another woman) Atwood. Though using the quotations of others in one's own poems is a device that may be intended to elevate the poet who "borrows," such quotations also pay homage to those who pass the art of poetry on. In this age of war piled on war, I applaud Berdeshevsky for including Siegfried Sassoon's deceptively offhand observation: *does it matter . . . losing your legs?*

Sassoon's quote burns a hole in the page, and Berdeshevsky writes:

> Who does not like heroes, come. The desert's stiffening. The weary camels under their trillion stars. I will not weep when I remember Zion. I will not stack pebbles.

In other similar poems she is cautionary, factual and convincingly ecstatic.

> To be drunk on the holy,
> on the holy spirit,
> on the owl,
> not afraid of any heat, not afraid of any day, or any
> night,
> a soul conducted,
> every portrait, holy,
>
> and joyous
> alone on a bicycle that does not belong to any-
> one. . . .

Ponsot writes that Berdeshevsky's "lines of elation are not free of the knowledge of suffering, just as her lines of suffering are not free of knowledge of elation." That balanced statement is high compliment. Berdeshevsky wears it with honor.

Hacker and Khoury-Ghata

Poets in a Time of War

In an interview with Annie Finch, Marilyn Hacker quotes the first line of a sonnet by Jamaican writer Claude McKay. "If we must die, let it not be like hogs." Later this sonnet, copied out in pencil, turned up in the pocket of a rebelling prisoner at Attica, and Hacker invokes the prisoner and McKay as examples of the isolated and disenfranchised who have seized on poetry in fixed forms to speak about their suffering. For those who may not be acquainted with Hacker's work, I offer this incident as a thumbnail portrait of a woman who wrote her first sonnet at age twelve, and at fifteen entered New York University. She is erudite in the best sense of that word, and politically engaged.

I've followed from its inception Hacker's career as a writer in fixed forms, beginning with *Presentation Piece*; taught *Assumptions* in graduate seminars in the Eighties; floated in the sonnet boats of *Love, Death and the Changing Seasons*; experienced political solidarity reading *Desesperanto*; and quoted for students her ironically All-American examples of an iambic pentameter line—"a double burger and a side of fries," or, if you'd prefer, "a glass of California Chardonnay."

Now comes *Names*, which foregrounds her passionate concern for the 20th and 21st Centuries' war victims, and her continuing engagement with form. In an online interview at How A Poem Happens, she describes her use of Hayden Carruth's invention of a form he called the "paragraph."

> The "paragraph," despite a name that makes it sound like a prose poem, is a fairly complex form. As Hayden Carruth used and described it, it is a fifteen-line poem, which, like a

sonnet, can either stand alone or work in sequence. It has a fixed rhyme scheme, and a fixed variation in the number of stresses per line. It is accentual rather than accentual-syllabic, though there is quite a bit of not-necessarily inadvertent iambic pentameter in most of them.

Asked if the poem is narrative, Hacker replies:

> There are several narratives and dialogues being negotiated here. The little girl in Gaza is at the heart of the poem, and yet she is cut off from "dialogue," telling her story and her indignation to an unseen interlocutor. The question of desire (and of disease) is left open-ended. The girl's anger, and the deliberately unspecified (not to embroider on a reality as far as I could observe it) situation reverberate from everything else evoked (including the language in which I might understand her) but remain painfully separate.

In poem after poem Hacker records her impressions of and friendships with other poets, prisoners and activists, female and male, living in "painfully separate" landscapes such as Gaza, Lebanon, Algeria, Russia under Stalin. The title poem features a linked series of portraits of women caught in war's net and evokes the impermanence of cultures breaking apart and disintegrating. Ours is a time "at the storm center of emergency / where there is no coherent narrative." Even ". . . the elegies get worn / away, attrition crumbles them. . . ." Our names, she writes, will be "erased, a cloud the wind dissolves. . . ."

Like Hacker, the women who appear in this eight sonnet sequence also write about women living through war. In Edinburgh airport Hacker bids farewell to a writer from Damascus, then concludes:

> I emailed her. I haven't heard from her.
> The war had started five days earlier.

Part four of this poem describes a restaurant gathering of "divergencies"—

> Palestinian Syrian, Lebanese,
> Russian, expat Jewish American.

The line following comments in strict iambic pentameter and understatement: "A new war had begun that afternoon."

Hacker also evokes war's frightening and dulling monotony with four bold iambs:

> Through the cracked prism of Al-Andalus
> we witness, mourning what we never had.
> (The war goes on and on and on and on.)

Imagine Hacker reading the *Manchester Guardian*, getting the news. Her subject is our world's disintegration, but she balances this with what is grounding—watching sunrise, drinking a glass of wine, the daily ritual of "letters typed on a computer screen." In the book's first section, Lauds, Hacker urges us to "inhabit daylight, unfurl where it's found / filtering through the curtain," and to enjoy "a dozen plump / oysters of hours, plate of a winter day / embossed with cloudy gilt chinoiserie." Though "disaster is inexorable somewhere," she counters with "dependable black coffee at Le Sancerre." The poems juxtapose polar opposites—embodiment and disintegration, creation and destruction. And though those daily coffees, those "letters typed on a computer screen" are anchorage, they are also ironic comment on the fact that war has become so prevalent as to seem ordinary, a staple like salt or milk.

We live with contradiction. In Ghazal: *dar al-harb* she laments the ambivalent nature of "my country" and its contradictory policies toward the rest of the planet. We are a nation of immigrants, and our government discriminates against immigrants. We are reputed to be a democracy and a hail-fellow-well-met people, and yet, Hacker opines,

> I might wish, like any citizen to celebrate my country
> but millions have reason to fear and hate my country.

She has mastered, out of necessity, the ironic lament:

> Where will justice and peace get the forged passports
> it seems they'll need to infiltrate my country?

Hacker will also be remembered for rendering nuanced portraits of women's lives. In a three-page poem about Anna

Akhmatova Hacker reminds us that women from all levels and classes still must invent their own flourishing, their sheer survival. She invokes Akhmatova's upper-class, privileged background, and also renders the difficulties faced by a prominent woman writer in Stalinist Russia.

> She and her friends and lovers chiseled lyrics
> until the decade (what did they think of revolution?)
> caught up with them, the elegant companions,
> and set them a different exercise.

Though Akhmatova hoped to secure her son's release from prison by writing poems praising Stalin, her son spent his youth in gulags. In a moment of bitterness, he called his mother "superficial." But the poem's final lines salute Akhmatova's quotidian perseverance beside thousands of other mothers.

> The impatient butterfly of Tsarskoye Selo,
> a solid matron, stood below the frozen
> walls, with her permitted package, like the others—
> whether they had been doting or neglectful mothers.

Hacker's description of Akhmatova as "solid" plays down whatever privilege she may have enjoyed, and aligns her with the women's classless dignity. And since perfect mothering is impossible, the final line's "doting or neglectful" reverberates as ironic—mothers, after all, are inevitably both.

Hacker can occasionally seem a bit arch, as in this aside:

> . . . (Over the ranch
> in Texas what smoke rises in premon-
> itory pillar?)

She also has a bag of favorite words which recur through her *oeuvre*—polyglot, maculate, divagations, exigent, pre-lapsarian, chinoiserie. Critics may skewer her for too often resorting to these familiars, but who would deny any writer the word "palimpsest"! Besides, she's absolved by the third section of "Paragraphs for Hayden," describing in simple language the six-year-old girl in Gaza beside an empty cradle of burnt blankets.

Hacker will be remembered for her instinct to balance what's fraught with what's grounding. Hence her nimble, graceful yoking of war, exile and the persistence of human hatred with our desire to witness sunrise and sunset, to tear a bite of bread from the loaf. She's a crier of disaster, who then reminds us of our comforts: kettle and cup, light and descending dark, some wine, a pen. She renders life's in-breaths and out-breaths, and, in accepting both, she walks the Middle Way.

Read Hacker's masterful translation of *Nettles: New and Selected Poems* by Lebanese novelist and poet Venus Khoury-Ghata. Born in northern Lebanon in 1937, she now lives in France and has published twenty novels and sixteen collections of poetry. *Nettles* contains poems from an earlier collection and a new sequence, "The Darkened Ones," written during Israel's 2006 war on Lebanon.

Khoury-Ghata's novels may best be characterized as metafiction, meaning they contain authorial asides which comment on the writing process. "Blackening pages till words exhaust themselves and this character emerges, whom I'm seeing for the first time," she writes. "I park him in the middle of the line / between a verb and an object." A second character

> . . . isn't long in coming
> It's visible in the ripples that ruffle the line
> He slips you the password NETTLES to make my task easier

Then Khoury-Ghata announces a third character:

> your main character
> the one who holds the strings, on whom everything
> converges

This third character is based on Khoury-Ghata's dead mother, a woman "in her faded apron / a washrag in one hand / her dignity in the other."

> An old woman bent right down to the ground pulls out with
> her bare hands
> the nettle which has sprouted on the page, then throws it in
> the margin. . . .

Death, Hacker writes in the introduction to *Nettles,* "becomes another mode of life, an ironic one carried on six feet below our surfaces." This dead mother's house has "a door but no walls / a wind but no windows." In this real yet imaginary burial ground, the old woman pulls up nettles, those "old acquaintances / acrimonious neighbors lacking all grace whom she took in out of charity."

This "was yesterday / it was long ago. . . . it was elsewhere," the text asserts. The old woman is dead, but like Garcia-Marquez suspending time's fixed perimeters, Khoury-Ghata places her characters in a floating landscape where verities don't hold, and populates this dreamscape with surreal imagery.

> A long time ago
> she owned a house with its plot of ocean
> a roof with its share of wind
> There were seagulls instead of a dog

Khoury-Ghata comments in an authorial aside describing war's camouflage language.

> I say knowledge so as not to say terror
> so as not to say retreat underground.

The dead, she tells us, "nourish themselves on the smell of our bread, drink the steam rising from our water, live on our noises." Having established this shifting terrain, she describes the Palestinian diaspora in Lebanon as "men who came from the wounded side of the river, knocked on our borders. . . ."

> They arrived every night of every year
> Their trees on leashes
> Their children planted at the foot of their olive trees
>
> . . . .
>
> They dug their trenches in our bedrooms
> Stretched their rifles out in our beds
> Squatted our sidewalks for the length of a man's life
> For the length of shame

Nettles' one new sequence, The Darkened Ones, is twenty haunting pages written during the 2006 war.

> We had shut ourselves out of the air's shapeless space
> for a ground eager to fill its hollows with
> bones rags barking

The Darkened Ones were

> . . . treated like ghosts
> entitled to use only the sound of light
> the shadow of noise
> a door in a drawing.

Khoury-Ghata honors the verbal shape-shifting characteristic of Arabic tales, and compares this to Magic Realism where "angels may converse with sign-painters and a pomegranate tree hang about a housewife's back door like a recalcitrant child." The dreamscape imagery arouses pathos.

> No one here helps a fallen house to get up
> No one wrings out flooded gardens

Her description of war-ravaged earth as abandoned wasteland where disembodied shades wander is affecting. Though the language of dreamscape buffers us from the poem's emotional rending, we feel pulled forward by the imagery's beauty, rising to meet the poem's intensity. This, Khoury-Ghata, tells us, is what war feels like. She would take us by the hand and say, This is suffering, see it in all its extravagant degradation, but remember also the spiritual realm and its balm. "They say the glaciers are heartless," she writes, "but they melt at the mere sight of a daisy." Hail to this driven writer's fluidity where "a white silk blouse flaps its wings."

Ingrid Wendt

Nonviolent Woman Warrior

There's a bittersweet irony in the fact that those writers most disturbed by violence seem driven to follow its scat unceasingly. In 1980 the poet and World War II conscientious objector William Stafford chose Wendt's first collection, *Moving the House,* for BOA Editions, recognizing in her work an echo of his own preoccupation with violence—a recognition that fueled their friendship until he died in 1993.

"Violence is a failure of the imagination," Stafford said, and Wendt is a writer whose oeuvre continues to probe the relation between imagination and violence in ways Stafford would have appreciated. I imagine him feeling sympathetic kinship with her as he read "Remembering Breughel's 'Massacre of the Innocents,'" in which she describes

> the mothers pleading, the children
> lying in blood, in snow, in a huge commotion of lances,
> hooves, dogs, the wails of the children, the mothers
> helpless with blood on their laps, on their hands,
> their eyes turned back from Heaven.

The agony in Breughel's image stands as Wendt's trademark. Hers is the charge of the serious artist confronting the engagement of perfection versus imperfection, justice versus injustice, violence versus tenderness. Hers is the ongoing agony of politics. Both Stafford and Wendt would agree with Polish Nobel Prize poet Wisława Szymborska, who, in "Children of Our Age," reminds us that, whether we like it or not, politics is ubiquitous.

. . . Whatever you say reverberates,
Whatever you don't say speaks for itself.
Either way you're talking politics.

Even when you take to the woods
you're taking political steps
on political grounds. . . .

The most political issue of all in the twenty-first century may well be what Stafford called "our common ground," meaning the planet suffering through climate change and the destruction of whole species. In *Singing the Mozart Requiem,* Wendt's second collection, the poem "Endangered Species" is much more than an evocative description of wild turkeys. "Endangered Species" is a political term which highlights the fact that the violence of species depletion is violence visible only in statistics. Wendt highlights the extremity of species' deaths by a cunning use of the words "if" and "as if"—"if" through the body of the poem, "as if" at the poem's conclusion. Notice how "if" builds a chain of linked contingencies.

If I had been five minutes later, or ten,
earlier, or hadn't gone down the lane for mail, the fields
of alfalfa ripe with robins, a fresh crop of grasshoppers

If the coyote flashing through one chance lift
of my head from a book, in broad daylight, hadn't
gone the wrong way, detoured by one rabbit less

Or the bear whose track I found on my way back
fresh and unmistakable as a blinking red light,
had staked out in just the right place, I might

never have seen the pause of wild turkeys under
the shelter of pines: aloof, the eternal
black robes of mourning; steady as county fair targets

one by one leisurely along
the edge of the field, the creek, up the hill into trees,
the edge of extinction beyond

all powers of observation. Purposeful.
As if there were others to take their place.
As if all of us had all the time in the world.

Wendt memorized Stafford's "A Ritual to Read to Each Other," in which he writes: "the signals we give—yes, or no, or maybe— / should be clear: the darkness around us is deep." It is because of this darkness that politics becomes her antagonist. In the introduction to her collection *The Angle of Sharpest Ascending* (2004) she writes: "Born in the last year of the Second World War to parents who had grown up speaking German to their families in Michigan and Chile, but who did not speak it in our Illinois home, I did not, until adolescence, begin to wonder why."

Wendt interrogates violence from the point of view of a nonviolent warrior fiercely confronting World War II's history. *The Angle of Sharpest Ascending* is composed in four, long, poem sequences: "I. Learning the Mother Tongue," "II. Suite for the Spirit's Geometry," "III. Questions of Mercy," and "'IV. Memory/ Memorial': Theme and Variations."

The four sequences address the Holocaust and the larger question of our human response to violence. In section 11 of "Learning the Mother Tongue" Wendt's musical instinct is to ground herself in the ballast and comfort of chant: "What cannot be spoken / what cannot be heard / Sharp instant of knowing / No substitute word . . . ." And later: "Silent as footsteps / That cannot be sung / What will not be recognized / Severs the tongue. . . ."

The Holocaust is background and sounding board in which each sequence reverberates backward and forward. The book's third sequence, "Suite for the Spirit's Geometry," arose through Wendt's collaboration with painter Traude Lindhart and sculptor Susi Rosenberg. Their cooperative venture energizes Wendt's quest to come to terms with the Holocaust, and in their company she examines the shreds of our moral rubble. In the first part of this sequence, sub-titled "Overture," Wendt speaks.

I, too, love
spatial constructions: together we speak

of tension, counterpoint, play
    of word on word, the spirit's

geometry. . . .

And in the fourth, untitled, section of "Suite for the Spirit's Geometry," Wendt analogizes from the Holocaust's violence to her own experience of America's Vietnam War.

> . . . our windmills of memory bring them up to the surface
> again and again: the girl on the campus green, kneeling over
>   the
> classmate inexplicably dead; the naked child running
>
> forever toward us, burning in napalm; the place you
>   remember
> being, exactly, and what you were doing the moment you
>   heard
> your leader was shot. How you passed the time
> until he was dead.

Wendt demands accountability, demands answers. But as Stafford wrote, "the answers are inside the mountains." And for Wendt poetry is the trail into the mountains. In *The Angle of Sharpest Ascending*'s final sequence, she emerges as a frank, fearless, spiritual cartographer leading us through the aftermath of violence, speaking truth to violence via the power of chant.

> Pillar of cloud, pillar of fire, beacon out of yesterday's
>   bondage
> Pillar of salt, pillar of stone, counsel not to look back upon
>   . . . .

Wendt has called up both material and spiritual realms in poems that deliver the heft of hewn stone and the lift of blown glass.

Had she not lived through the fiery inquisition of *The Angle of Sharpest Ascending,* it would have been impossible for Wendt to write the poems in *Surgeonfish.* Now there is an earned and easeful sophistication in her interrogation of violence. The six-page poem "Questions of Grace" is the most detailed, nuanced work I know of on the near impossibility of a benign vegetarianism. Through the poem's twelve sections she provides instance after instance, in which, by refraining from causing harm in one instance we inadvertently cause harm in another. Thus she concludes, "Reader, what / day do we not trade / at least one voice for our own?"

Surgeonfish is rich with examples of engagement with the natural landscape. These engagements gather into a mosaic, some of which are portraits of encounters with live creatures: being "whacked on the head by a great horned owl" protecting its young; the porcupine at dusk taking five minutes to cross the road, to which she responds: "The slowest beauty can rush me." In contrast, the rollicking sestina "Road Kills," a smart, ironic take on accidental (oh I'm so sorry!) vs. deliberate (you had it coming, babe!) murder—smartly showcases America's bloodthirsty unconscious.

"You create a good poem," Stafford said, "by revising your life, . . . living the kind of life that enables good poems to come about." And Wendt has achieved that balance in which the life of the mind and of the heart wisely bow to each other. In poem after poem in *Surgeonfish* and in its sequel *Evensong,* she evokes her relation to the natural world with an appealing authenticity. "Poem at Forty-Five" finds her in the live, green world, honoring spider webs.

> . . . each morning I find them
> beautiful, go
>
> out of my way to lift, lightly, at least
>
> one nearly invisible polar thread to another,
> safer anchor: each
>
> shimmer, flat, before-Columbus plate of the world
>
> adrift: wheels
> within wheels
> and the motionless sun at the center,

a solstice
poised in its own
readiness . . . . . .

In "Requiem for a Soprano" she invokes music as a path to transcendence, comparing the soprano's voice to millions of icebergs glittering on blue water

. . . as though God has taken
a giant finger over the water's surface, whirled it white,
a whole new galaxy, too

vast to be named. Song
could get lost in a space like this.

Or fill it. . . .

Again and again the natural world is made vivid in these poems, and Wendt addresses our connection with this world's web and with each other. In "Mother's Day, Ellensburg, Washington" she declares the necessity of keeping "this inescapable human circle in repair. . . ."

. . . why am I suddenly grateful . . .
in the store when a clerk I'd never met, exclaimed

What a beautiful jacket! and I saw she was talking to me.
And why, less than an hour ago, asking directions of the older-
than middle-aged filling station attendant, didn't I follow
my impulse to ask where she got that peach-colored orchid on

her lapel, so she could maybe have told me one of her children
gave it to her. . . .

But the most startling poem—compelling for its combining of the earthly and the transcendent—is "Benediction." In a series of tercets Wendt describes washing her mother's body for burial. "Benediction" ought to have been published by *Poetry,* or the *New Yorker* or the *Atlantic,* and flagged for a Pushcart Prize. Is it poetry politics that's kept this work from thousands of readers who would be in awe of Wendt's art and richly comforted by it?

Evensong also revisits Wendt's and Stafford's address to violence. In the poem "Numbers," a poem that will end with a line borrowed from Stafford, she enumerates the death count of war's casualties: airline disasters, mass graves, earthquake, tsunami, the Twin Towers. Citing the numbers of the dead won't a poem make, and citing the numbers of those who rallied against "Shock and Awe" won't a poem make either. Nor will citing the subsequent numbers of the dead, the maimed. But Wendt perseveres, as though, in her passion for justice, she would force numbers to speak.

Find a way to sing it, I wanted to say. But what I didn't know was that she was writing toward a crucial quote by Pete Seeger, a quote which sets up the last line of the poem, which is the quote from Stafford. "Here's how to count the people who are ready to do right: 'One.' 'One.' 'One.'"

It's a defiant line, it's Stafford's line, and it erases my impatience with those awful numbers by translating them into human anguish. But the genius of the poem is Wendt's. She's borrowed brilliantly, and delivered resounding homage to her mentor.

When Stafford died in 1993, Wendt established an annual celebration in Eugene, Oregon, every January at which poets read Stafford poems. In a 2011 essay written in honor of her mentor, "The Unknown Good in Our Enemies: The Poetry of William Stafford and Poetry from the Middle East," she cites the First World War's spontaneous 1914 Christmas truce. Along the Western Front thousands of German and British troops walked toward each other across no man's land, shouting greetings, fraternizing, offering each other food, alcohol and tobacco.

It was Stafford who remarked that violence is a failure of imagination, but it's Wendt who evokes this stunning example of imagination's transcendent power—enemies spontaneously coming together in solidarity. She takes her place in the poetry canon with honor, as her mentor would have wished.

VI.

Poetry and the Healing Arts

Poetry and the Healing Arts

Collaboration

Hasina: veil of skin, draped over bone. So thin she can't walk, sit up, hold a cup. Eyes a single beam, scanning for food, even when she's full. If I cover the woman next to Hasina with a sheet, Hasina wants to be covered. If I bring another woman a biscuit between meals, Hasina demands a biscuit, hides it under her mattress. If another calls for water, Hasina too signals, waving her hand.

Flashback to my first meeting with Jean Watson, Dean of the University of Colorado's School of Nursing. When Emma Goldman said "Pettiness separates, breadth unites: let us be broad and big," she might have been describing this visionary nurse-theorist. She'd established the Center for Human Caring on the campus, and brought in musicians, philosophers and alternative healers. She perceived poetry not as arty entertainment but as a perceptive tool that might portray nursing in its complex fullness. She invited me to serve as Artist in Residence at the Center and to write poems that would render nurses' emotional dynamics with patients in a vivid, compelling way.

"Health care's become dominated by technology," she said, "and we need the humanities to show the human side."

I was intrigued. "Why not a journalist?"

"Journalism won't capture what we do," she said. "We need the arts. I want someone like yourself who'll see us in ways we can't see ourselves. Whatever you see will be useful to us."

In the course of that year I spent one day a week observing midwives, psychiatric nurses, community health nurses who made home calls, nurses in ICUs, Burn Units, cancer wards and surgery. Nursing is a collaboration in which two people need each other. Without the wounded and ill, nurses would have no object, and in a similar fashion the sick depend on nurses' finely tuned sensibilities and their nuanced experience of hurt, recovering beings. The two collaborate with each other, and now I became part of those collaborations. My poems would reflect subjective reality as I perceived it while being a part of it.

In the realm of the body which is also the realm of the soul, I witnessed and was enlarged by the give-and-take of interdependence in which two beings become "one." When we're sick, we don't care about the latest improvement on the laparoscope. We're hurt animals, and we want to be recognized, comforted, reassured. Amidst intimidating steel bed rails, drips, tubes and charts, the urgency of patients' needs blends with nurses' instincts. On one occasion a nurse was to bathe a quadriplegic man. He'd been lifted into the tub by two strong orderlies. Now he told her he didn't want a bath. She spoke to him, indicating by gesture and attitude that the decision was his. But as she began to walk away, he called her back. He'd changed his mind.

"You have to let them keep their dignity," she told me, "however they define it."

Browsing a medical textbook, I learned that human skin is classified as an organ. An adult's skin, if you were to flay it, would weigh six pounds and cover eighteen square feet. I was stunned by the text's cold matter-of-fact delivery. My response was to counteract my sense of disembodiment by weaving this chilly data into the warmth of a poem.

As the year progressed, I kept writing, revising, fine-tuning. Some situations I cast in third person to capture the "invisible" work nurses do by sketching nurse and patient from a distance. Others I wrote as monologues, constructing an epos that conveyed in a nurse's first-person voice her inner world.

Because many health care professionals are not accustomed to reading poetry, and because *Midwife* would become a text in nursing schools across the country, the NLN editor suggested that I write brief prose introductions to each of the collection's five sections. This seemed fitting, for though we think of poetry and prose as different mediums, we speak in both "languages." Thus I wrote the following prose introductions as prose poems.

Celebration of the Body

> Our bodies are our world. They are both end and means for us. In the body we live and move and have our being. In the body we have our comedy and our tragedy, joys and sorrows. We recognize the body as our instrument through which we live out our existence. In caring for others and in accepting care from others we feel the spiritual community which can only take place in this world, in the flesh. "Skin" rejects the Puritan ethic of denying, subduing, and suppressing the body, and treats the skin, an organ through which we communicate with each other, as eminently worthy of praise. "Skin" ventures even further, arguing that touch is not only essential to physical well being, but that this tactile communication, or lack of it, has psychological, social and profoundly political consequences as well.

In another introduction I used the metaphor of food and feeding to describe the relationship between caregivers and their patients.

Food as Power / Power as Food

> Power as we know it in relations between people is as basic as food. It is like food in its effect on us. Using our power to give to another person is like feeding that person. Taking what someone else offers is like eating. Many are the ways in which we can feed each other, and all of us flourish and are at our best when we manage not to share power but to share in it. When we feed and are fed by each other, power becomes the fluid essence of the universe, that which is in us all and which belongs to no one.

But food and feeding are sometimes used as tools of aggression in power relationships. On a global scale the rich nations which we call "world powers" are in a position to give or refuse food and other kinds of care to poor nations. Governments take a similar position in regard to their constituents. And on an individual level a parent has the power to give or refuse food and care to a child.

Caregivers, however, understand that their relationships with patients are reciprocal. No one is human alone. A patient wanting to die may be kept alive by technology, "maintained" in a physical state technically referred to as "alive." But this person does not "live." The will to live, the choice to live, is a personal one. The patient and no one else possesses this will. Thus caregivers must continuously assess the person's perception of his or her own will. And the caregiver must remind the person of his or her own dignity, recognize that dignity and allow it.

The caregiver's power is the power to bring forth what the patient already possesses: free choice and personal desire. In this situation power is not an exclusive possession of one at the expense of another, but is an atmosphere in which two become a community, become "one."

My poem "Commerce City: *Los Pobres*" makes clear that the caregiver is not simply a professional but a person multiple and varied, complicated and needy. The caregiver who "feeds" others is also "fed" by them, and she understands and welcomes this, and recognizes this exchange as an essential fact of the process of care. The relationship between caregiver and patient is mutual, and their giving and receiving extends beyond them into the community, and both are satisfied by their multiplied mutuality.

Commerce City: Los Pobres

Imagine the angels of bread.
Martin Espada

Commerce City, grit
thickening the air, and you can't
get a job here, not

much of one, and if you do it will
kill you. The drone of the interstate
is the sound of

monotony. The word sounds like
poverty, and is. The roofs
of the greenhouses glitter

like rhinestones. Beneath the tinny lids
of shacks, in the dimness
babies are sprouting. I know

where to go. The dogs
know me, little boys take my hands,
their chatter the sound

color would make
if it spoke. In their mouths
my name is a green

blur, a whirr in blue
air, as though I too
have come far, leaving

an equator, bringing what I could
carry. Here at the door
good smells: Castenga

will feed me—*posole, frijoles,* braid
straight down her
spine, and the radio

on. Castenga's orange skirt the light
we see by, babies a covey of quail
at her feet. Now she holds out

the new one, talking bright talk
to this boy, the bulb
of a lily, fat with its

juices. She is proud of this
fifth one, though her veins ache
and her feet hurt, and there's

not enough sleep to go around. How he
glistens—oiled and round as an
olive, and already, pinned

to his nightshirt, a silver medal
against evil. For there are
evil spirits, I too believe this,

I have seen them strike the living down
again and again, and before
their prime. You do what you can

against evil, you feed those who
fight it, you give them
a bed and your blankets, what

talismans against it
you have. Now I take this boy
against me. This is how it

is here, someone offering me
something good to eat or to hold.

Violence and Dignity

Human dignity is both as present as a steel girder and as vulnerable as a butterfly's wing. It can be a powerful personal tool, and it can be destroyed by a casual remark. It can be snuffed out by physical violence and by overt and subtle, insinuating forms of psychological violence. We can recognize and affirm dignity in ourselves, and deny or affirm it in others. This power to deny or affirm is not necessarily limited by class, race or economic status. Anyone can acknowledge and respect or ignore and deny the dignity of another.

Dignity is essential to health. Without it we do not flourish. Without attention to it, an injured person may not heal. In "Quadriplegic: The Bath" I've highlighted not just the absence of violence in the caregiver's manner, but also her active affirmation of another's human "being." The caregiver openly concedes power to the man, confirming his dignity, saluting the virility he still possesses.

Quadriplegic: The Bath

"You'll feel like
new," I said, keeping things
breezy, as though we all know
how getting clean feels
good—no one in their right mind
would refuse it, because he looked
like he just might file
a dissenting opinion. Which he could

do. Though he couldn't get up and
go—bye, Sugarbuns, I'm walkin' out
on you—which is what he'd have

liked to do. He leaned back then, the old
stinker, like Caesar in his chariot, and let me
see his penis, that loose fold of flag
that would not fly again, and said,
"M'am, you seem to have the wrong
man. I don't require either your services
or your opinions." I could see

how indeed neither service nor opinion
would be of the slightest use
to him. "O.K., all right," I said,
hand across forehead in mock shock,
letting him know the sharpness of the male
was in him still. "O.K.," I said, "I get
the picture." And I turned and was
going, leaving him the privacy
he had once, like a general, commanded. "Oh hell,"
he said, and with a sweep of his head, drew me in.
"You'll catch it if you don't do me. Anyway,
I stink. Come on with your scrub brush." So I knelt
beside the water the orderlies had set him in
and began to bathe him.

Moral Baptism

Does a fetus have rights? What rights do prospective parents have? Should individuals be allowed to choose to die? Should caregivers assist them? Is a caregiver's obligation to treat patients even against the patient's wishes? The poems in this section articulate only a few of the more obvious attitudes toward ethical issues. "Burn Unit: Baptist" presents one person's reaction to extreme pain.

Burn Unit: Baptist

These women say it's pain I feel,
but it's the fire. How complete it is,
like the way, when you're a kid,
they describe God: He is always

With you. I am everywhere open
to his probing fingers. It's never
about to begin, and it's never over,
it's now, and He never sleeps, and

I can't walk away. Everything stops
except the fire: it's the fire that's
Everlasting. These women keep me
breathing, they feed me through a

tube, they feed me and feed me
and think they're doing good—
I see, through the blur heat makes
in the air, their conviction. They

think what they do is an act
of compassion. They believe
they love me. What they don't
understand is that feeding the fire

keeps it going. Once you're
burning, it goes on and on,
until someone who can
puts the fire out.

Metaphysics

Over and over I watched a caregiver and the person receiving care come to constitute one wholeness. When two of us enter into each other willingly and receptively, the gestalt of our separate beings loosens and vibrates. The material of our being and becoming begins to flow. We experience ourselves and each other as elemental substance. We experience the living field of our interconnectedness. And we fill with energy, a living material, palpable. This energy is visible in the air around us. It's as though we give off light.

These moments of transcendence occur again and again, each time flowering forth intense energy and material presence.

I felt I was witnessing the invisible made substance. I was witnessing the spirit made flesh. "Midwife" suggests the vast resources, the complexity, the nuanced intelligence and the power of the caregiver at work in the metaphysical realm.

Midwife

for Jean Watson

Though I seem to wait
I'm moving at the speed of light

Though I seem to stand by
I'm running easily over the windswept grasslands
to where the river divides the plains from the mountains

Though I seem to stand by
I'm gathering the sweet and the bitter herbs
in shade and in sunlight
I'm digging out the bones of the lost animals
embedded in the lakes of tar

Though I seem idle
I'm releasing the father's fear into the wind,
watching the wind disperse it

Though I seem idle
I'm sending the mother, wave by wave, the energy
of the deep and of the shallow waters

Though I seem idle
I'm traveling by night and by day, over earth and over sea
to meet the new being

When I time the contractions
I'm counting the sheaves of grain
gathered in the mother's harvest

When I measure the opening
I'm calculating the number of followers
in the mother's fields

And when I touch the father's shoulder
I'm singing the many names
of the ancestors who overcame fear

When I seem to pause
I send light to the father, the mother, the older sister

When I seem to pause
I send light to those who will wash and wrap the new being.

When I listen to the heartbeat of the new being coming
I hear the thud of the rapids upriver

When I listen to the heartbeat of the mother
I hear the tumbling of water down a great falls

When I lean forward, hands cupped for the head,
I'm dividing the wind into the four directions

When I lean forward, hands cupped for the head,
I'm gathering together the rain and the desert heat

And when at last I hold the head in my hands
I've hoisted the sun to the pinnacle of the heavens

When I hold the new being in my hands
I've brought mother, father and child
into the center of the eleven sacred circles

And when I lay the new being on the mother's breast
I'm sending flocks of goats to graze on hillsides and in the valleys
I'm setting the fish loose at the headwaters of the rivers
I'm letting the birds go into the great migrations

When I clamp the cord in two places
I'm saying the child's two names,
one from the mother, one from the father

When I give the father the tool to cut the cord
    I'm binding three people together
    until the death of the last of the three

When I take the print of the new being's foot
    I'm writing in the ancient alphabet the word just uttered

When the placenta comes and I examine the placenta
    I'm sorting the particles and waves in the spectrum of
        light

And when my work is done and I go from the place of birth
    I walk out across the fields of the planets
    Into the spaces between the furthest stars

Thanks to the nurses I worked with, the poems embodied a persuasiveness that caught the public's attention. Poetry was a lens that began to elevate the status of nurses in the public's mind. Nursing schools began using *Midwife* as a text, and the discerning public began to perceive nurses as prestigious figures. It was gratifying to feel that I'd helped turn the wheel of their earned elevation and prominence in the public sphere. Though we did not know it at the time, we'd helped launch a movement in which nurses and physicians themselves would write their personal stories of "the medical experience" and learn with and from each other.

Think of me, reader, as someone learning to bow. I became a candle wick that's dipped again and again in the warm wax of soul. In that year of accompanying nurses I was reminded again and again that the way up the mountain is down—on your knees. I'd seen patients humbled by their faltering bodies, and I too had been humbled, reminded that life is not a right but a privilege, that I am dependent on the generosity of the world around me.

Collaborative relationships are at the heart of the human condition. I interviewed and wrote portraits of a sound healer, a medicine woman, a *curandera*. So when I flipped on T.V. and saw Mother Teresa in Calcutta at her Kalighat Home for the Destitute and Dying, I wanted to go there and work in that circle of care.

Yesterday is gone, Mother Teresa said, *and tomorrow has not yet come. We have only today. Let us begin.* Swirled in Calcutta's Diesel-filled air, trucks and lorries crowded the thoroughfares, revving their engines, grinding huge gears. Every day thousands of refugees arrived from Bangladesh. People fought over taxis, and on the bus I stood—the seats reserved for women were already taken. This was a July rife with contagion, and citizens on the streets were coughing, sneezing, feverish. Even so, I boarded the bus and was happy through the forty-minute ride to Kalighat. Again and again the bus stalled in traffic, but I was game.

At Kalighat there was none of the West's expensive and intimidating medical equipment. The daily routine centered on bare essentials: meals, baths, the changing of linens, the agape of an embrace. There was only a small supply of antibiotics—Mother Teresa depended on the public's donations—and mostly what we had to offer were vitamins and pain killers. The most technological procedure was a drip hanging from a coat tree.

Those here knew they were dying, and death was a common occurrence. Volunteers served food, gave baths, emptied bedpans, changed soiled clothing. Washing fifty-four plastic mattress covers on the women's ward each day was hard work, and when I needed to debrief, there was writing. All my life I'd taken part in the private collaboration between the writer and the world. Now, in the ongoing conversation poetry was, I could spoke freely and wildly.

When Hasina arrived, I guessed she was in her thirties. In Bengali she told Sister Luke she was fourteen. Then she stopped speaking. Now that she was in a safe place, she was overwhelmed by her suffering. Every day I bathed and fed her, gave her vitamins, held her hand, stroked her. One day she began to moan. Sister Luke asked her in Bengali where she hurt. Hasina shook her head. Luke threw up her hands and went to see about another woman's drip. Hasina looked at me, her eyes anguished. Her moaning was a rhythmic utterance. I knelt beside her and sat her up. But she couldn't stay upright alone. So I put my arms around her, and we climbed onto the rhythm of her moaning and began to rock.

Six o'clock came, and the other volunteers left. The light lowered toward dusk, and the nuns went upstairs to prepare their evening meal. Around us the other women dozed. I closed my eyes. I had nowhere to get to. The only sounds were the nearby whir of a fan, Hasina's moan. I was content to rock with Hasina, and there came a moment when rocking her was also rocking me. We rocked each other, and kept on rocking, and then came a moment when everything dissolved. I was no longer myself but a wave of energy, which was also Hasina's wave, and I couldn't tell myself from Hasina, from the fan's whir, the encompassing air.

Beautiful Trouble

The first time I see Mother Teresa striding down the hall, it's clear that she has let go all pointless baggage. She's short and wide, she has energy in spades, and she barrels on like a tank. She can't be stopped. She comes to chapel early, kneels on the back, right-hand corner mat, and gets busy praying.

The room where mass takes place is spare—a simple altar, floor mats for the nuns, bare floor for those who have come to work at Kalighat, where the destitute come to die. The priest comes in last. His voice is the call, ours the response. Through high windows fiery light pours down, the room fills with lifting energy, and our words fly up and out the windows like a flock of doves. I imagine that nothing my hand touches will ever again be hard, cold matter.

Calcutta in July is a Petri dish multiplying microbes. Sidewalks fill with sneezing, coughing citizens. Lorries crowd thoroughfares, revving engines, grinding huge gears, and I sweat, cough, sneeze with the multitudes. The hospice is next door to a Kali temple. Did Mother Teresa choose Kalighat's location because Kali Ma, the Hindu triple goddess of creation, preservation, destruction would reside next door?

I arrive as Sister Luke instructs a young Brit man to get down on his hands and knees and scrub the entrance threshold. Roughly half the volunteers are in their forties or fifties, and the others, like this Oxford undergrad, are the young who aspire to change the world. Would Sister Luke admit that she likes seeing this privileged boy on his knees?

I introduce myself, and Sister Luke nods.

"Women work on women's ward," she says, pointing.

Luke goes back to her desk on a raised platform between

the men's and women's wards, and records the new donation of Bactrim in her ledger. Thus ends my training. Karin who is my age shows me where to find supplies of clean gowns, sheets, towels, soap, points out the bathing area, toilets. The only medical apparatus is a handful of thermometers and one drip bottle hung from a coat rack. There's a cabinet of meds, mostly over-the-counter painkillers—and that's it. But this bare simplicity doesn't feel austere. I have friends in the states who are nurses, and I recognize the atmosphere they mysteriously create with their presence. Kalighat houses the harrowing of illness and death, and it's also the harboring landscape of love.

As a child I'd played beneath an elm next to my grandmother's yellow irises. Into this bower I brought abandoned things—a fallen blossom, a dying cricket, pebbles that called me. A cracked saucer of rainwater. I'd cherished these forgotten ones, and played at comforting them. I suspect that this play was a way of assuring myself that I would also be comforted.

Here I go the rounds from seven a.m. to two, collecting more of the world's abandoned. *Unless we participate in the dread, the sense of loss, the anguish, the dereliction and the destitution of the crucified,* wrote Thomas Merton, *we cannot enter into the mystery:* the mystery of the interconnection between all things. We are not always aware of this interconnection. But when we notice it, to participate in others' pain makes obvious sense.

Karin asks Sister Luke where she keeps the shrouds.

"You are here three days," Luke says, "and you do not know where are shrouds?"

The windows are above our heads: they afford privacy but let in light. The cots are low, so I must kneel, and the lower you go, the less high and mighty you can pretend to be. I can't understand Bengali, nor can my language be understood. And how fitting—for I'm in a place where my actions will speak louder than words. I mime: shall I carry you to the bath? Help you walk to the latrine? Do you want a cup of water? A woman nods: yes, please. Another pushes the glass away. When they chat with each other do they assess me? It doesn't matter.

Kneeling beside their cots, I'm bowing to them. I practice this bow the way I practiced the piano over and over. The women are the black and white keys, the possibility of love's music. Some are starved, some worn down by the hard work of living without wealth. I fill their cups with water and remember myself at four, working in the garden with my mother. Afterward we bathed together, and my mother looked weary but happy. Work was a glass of elixir, and she'd drunk it down. Her body's satisfaction was a kind of wealth. Now her body is giving in like the bodies of these women. Like Calcutta's old mansions that once were grand, they're crumbling.

In the nineteenth century the Bengali elite built their palaces in Calcutta, the culture flourished, and the poet and mystic Rabindranath Tagore recited his astonishing poems. Now Mother Teresa's work has pumped up Calcutta's prestige again. She bows to this city every afternoon between three and four, when she opens the door of her private quarters and steps out to receive anyone who comes.

The new French volunteer Clarice is just out of high school, and aspires to become a nun. As a first step while still in Paris she'd shaved her head.

"Come with me to visit Mother. Please! I am too frightened to go alone!"

I remember the hot feel of idolatry when I was four: my mother, I believed, was the repository where all the secrets were kept. Clarice is in idolatry's grip, and ardor like hers, in someone so young, is sweet. We bus to the Motherhouse and join the line of supplicants waiting. At three Mother opens her door, steps out, greets the first petitioner. The line moves slowly as each supplicant departs floating above the parquet.

Clarice is nervous. Will meeting Mother bring on palpitations? Fainting, it occurs to me, is very French. Does Clarice carry smelling salts in the pocket of her lacy cotton blouse? A family of five Bengalis in front of us takes their turn.

Clarice clutches my forearm. "Mother is so close!" she whispers.

The five hustle off, and Clarice sinks to her knees at Mother's feet. Mother grips her arm and tugs her up. Clarice is in shock: forbidden to kneel? This cannot be! Again she collapses. Again Mother tugs her arm: there will be no groveling!

"What is your name?" Mother asks. "Where are you from?"

Clarice is weak from the strain of being gazed upon by a saint. "Paris!" she gasps.

Mother explains that the Sisters of Charity operate AIDS hospices all over France, and urges Clarice to volunteer when she returns. Clarice nods vigorously. Mother has instructed her how to proceed in life! Clarice holds out a tiny St. Teresa medal and presses it into Mother's hand. Mother's hand presses it back.

"I have taken a vow of poverty," Mother says. "I can't accept gifts."

Clarice is stricken. For months she has worn the medal on a chain at her throat and fantasized laying its slight weight in Mother's hand. Again Clarice offers it. Mother is cheery firmness: no. I chat a few moments with Mother, then turn Clarice toward the stairs. Clarice is teary with the triumph of success and the devastation of failure. Halfway down the staircase she stops and thrusts out the necklace.

"Please—please!—will *you* take it? I must give it to *someone*!"

My cough and runny nose subside, but heat and sweat go on. Every day thousands more Bangladeshi refugees arrive in Calcutta. People fight over taxis. While the bus hauls us through Diesel air, past corrugated tin shacks and small, faltering shops, I think of Boulder, Colorado. Our Pearl Street Mall is *Armani et al.* Get your designer socks here, twenty-five bucks a pair. Much attention goes to the politically correct purchase—not the cotton but the silk zafu and zabuton set. You glimpse the young man from Nuevo Laredo only as he's disappearing down a manhole to repair pipes. You see the restaurant's Nepalese busboy only on your way to the loo.

Now I'm the foreigner. When I step down from the bus, a beggar sits on the sidewalk, waiting. Take along your sense of humor, a friend warned me. You'll be a White Person, a mark for Calcutta's beggars—some of whom work for themselves and some for The Man. And how, I asked, will I tell true beggars from charlatans? You can't, my friend said, but that's o.k. Charlatans too need work.

Some of the volunteers have a beggar policy. Give to the first three, then stop. Put fifty rupees in your pocket and when it's gone, that's it. And don't give to children begging, because it encourages them to become lifetime beggars. I don't have a policy. Every day is a new day, and this beggar has one arm. He wears a ragged *Notre Dame* tee, and with his one arm holds out his bowl. I take a fistful of coins from my pocket, drop them in—the beggar bows—and I'm off down the street to Kalighat.

Indians know that when someone can no longer contribute to the family's income, you take that person to Calcutta's train station, confident that Mother Teresa's van will come, and the saint herself will take over. Today the van brings Salwari, the wife of a farmer. When she broke a leg, her husband couldn't afford to pay a doctor to set it. And when it healed, she was crippled and couldn't work in the fields. She became a mouth her family couldn't afford to feed. Now she has bedsores. She is in pain and has told Luke she hopes to die soon. She's stopped eating. Sister Luke cleans her sores, applies disinfectant. Salwari is stoic: not a wince.

"God," Luke says, disapproving, "is taking a long time."

My fourteenth day: simplicity is a monastery. Here where routine repeats there's no reason to hurry, and I see more clearly. Mid morning the van delivers Hasina. I guess that she's in her thirties. In Bengali she tells Luke she's fourteen. She's starving and too weak to sit up alone. She can't hold a cup. I carry her to the bathing stall, chatting in English on the theory that the sound of a voice is food. Then towel her, dress her, carry her back to the cot. I kneel and prop her up, lift a spoonful of curry. She is ravenous, eager for each bite, but she can't yet eat much at one time.

The distance between the hungry and the fed is the most vast distance there is. But hunger is also an altar where we learn to feed each other. The hungry and the fed, the starved and the fat: we are equals in need, the need to be loved and the need to love. Like a key and its lock, the hungry and the fed are designed to fit each other perfectly.

Feeding another person is the simplest of acts, and from this act, feeling begins to flow. When I feed Hasina, I am the generous and powerful giver, and at the same time some neglected part of me is also fed. The act of offering the spoon leads straight to the heart of the mystery—the mystery that in raising the spoon to her mouth, I fill us both.

Today Mother's van brings a woman beggar. Her skin is dark from days in the sun, and her eyes are infected, bound shut with puss. Her broken left hand has healed into a flesh corsage, permanently pinned above her left breast. Her right arm thrusts straight up to take the coins—and she can't lower this arm. The fingers of her thrust-up hand are clenched shut.

Luke speaks in Bengali. The woman utters a moan. "Bath," Luke says.

I peel off the woman's clothes, carry her slight body to the tub. Her moan is a low-volume drone. I bathe her shut eyelids and try to open her clenched fingers. But it's as though her fist has fused shut. I bathe her and talk to her quietly.

"I'll make you comfortable, I'll feed you. Don't worry, you're not alone."

She doesn't know my language, but she hears the tone of my voice, and by speaking to her, I also reassure myself. I carry her back to her cot, offer a spoonful of rice. She won't or can't eat.

I cover her with a thin sheet and go cot to cot with my pitcher, pouring the women drinks of water. We make little jokes. Sometimes a woman wants me to sit with her, hold her hand. Going among these flagging bodies reminds me that I too am vulnerable, I too will suffer. I keep one eye on the woman beggar. Her eyes are still shut.

I go to her and offer food again. Again she refuses.

Her moan is a sound worn thin, a drone.

I sit on the cot next to her. She needs to be held. So I sit her up, lay her one free arm around my neck, put both my arms around her. I hold her and rock us back and forth. She moans, and I moan in return. Back and forth, her moan, then mine. Then I switch, so that I moan when she moans. Our moan has become a song, and we climb on.

As we go on, our bodies breathe, and we loosen. We are less bodies now than vibrations coming in waves. No money changes hands, no one is counting. We inhabit the mesh of belonging and go on rocking. Then comes a moment when these waves of energy, mine and hers, are ours. I can scarcely tell myself from her, nor from the fan's whir stirring the air.

Salwari lies on her side. Luke swabs an open sore, but Salwari doesn't flinch. Luke is impatient: where is God? That's the powerful for you, she seems to say, never there when you need them. *God is present,* Simone Weil wrote, *at the point where the eyes of those who give and those who receive meet.* Salwari opens her eyes.

She looks at Luke. "I die soon."

I kneel beside two men from the men's ward, the three of us scrubbing sheets and towels by hand. There are many, many sheets, and we concentrate on scrubbing and fall silent: the only sound the swish of wet cloth, and beyond the high windows I hear the orchestra of traffic.

Space is at a premium in Calcutta, and the clotheslines are on the roof. We carry wet sheets up the stairs and hang them. Crows flap past, and the smoke of incense from the courtyard of the Kali temple wafts upward. Worshipers mill, and I spot two men in suits with briefcases. Also the baker from the shop on the corner. Women in saris appear, bells on their ankles. They join the priests circling Kali, shaking tambourines and chanting. I savor the sweet smell of clean clothes. This scent suggests the future in which I'll bathe and dress the women. In the meantime I remember that Kali's mouth is wide open, her fangs poised to bite.

I've been here three weeks, each day giving a beggar or two a little something. Today I made eye contact with a beggar and walked on. He leapt up and charged after me. I kept walking, but he ran and got in front of me, then turned obsequious, crawling on his knees, whining. When I ignored him, he stood and followed me down the street, shouting I know not what profanities. I felt beleaguered, then on the edge of fury. We were losing it, goading each other on. We created a situation intolerable to us both, and both of us had cooperated to construct this fierce standoff.

Suddenly it hit me: our anger was cooperative. We'd conspired together to be furious at each other. In an instant my anger dissolved, and I giggled. The beggar was startled. We paused, assessing each other. Then he too grinned. I reached into my pocket, drew out rupees equivalent to a couple of U.S. dollars, and offered them. He accepted, and bowed to me. When he rose, I bowed to him in return.

Hasina is hungry between meals. She speaks her one English word: *biscuit.* I get her one. She eats a bite, hides the rest beneath the mattress. Her eyes ravenous. An old woman complains of pain in her hip. I look for aspirin, Tylenol, codeine, but we're out. We're also out of tea.

When we run out of something, Mother Teresa is Kalighat's oil well. She prays and hustles, and that day or the next what we need comes. Hasina asks for another biscuit. I turn up my hands: no more left. Luke hails me.

"Come."

I follow her. She points to the beggar woman I'd rocked.

"Dress her in shroud."

No one I'm close to back in Boulder has died. I have no experience of the newly dead. Now I am in a place where death is common. And this woman and I have a history. In those moments of rocking each other we were two bodies become one being. I'd imagined the dead would be light. When I lift the woman's leg, it's heavy as stone. I maneuver, getting her body into the shroud. Then I ask Luke: is there a funeral ritual?

"Van takes them to Ganges. One priest is Catholic. He blesses those we bring."

The woman's fist is still clenched shut. I pry her fingers partway open, enough to see in her palm three *pais,* coins worth less than a penny.

I kiss her knuckles, take a breath and let it out. Let her go.

Today when I leave Kalighat the light lowers toward evening. The street leading to the main thoroughfare seems unusually quiet. Then I hear a communal shout. I edge through the throng standing along the curb. The boulevard has been cordoned off from traffic and is filled with ranks of barefoot pilgrims. They halt, kneel and prostrate themselves full frontal on the pavement. Then they rise, advance one step, and again prostrate themselves. After each prostration a Hindu priest chants a line. Those watching the pilgrims answer him with a collective shout.

Repetition reassures us that life goes on, and variation reminds us that our lives are constantly changing. Our bodies continuously slough off old cells and keep making new ones. In that way we are continuously appearing and disappearing. But we've learned to perceive ourselves and each other as solid bodies. Is the slow deliberateness of the pilgrims' prostrations another way to enter the mystery? Prostration by prostration the procession slowly moves on.

The month I signed on for is almost up, and I've settled in. I've imagined that leaving Calcutta will feel like a tearing. Now that day comes: I get off the bus and head to Kalighat. Not a beggar in sight. Did police do a sweep-up? Even if they did, they'd have missed someone. Men pass me heading to work, women to market, children to school, but no beggars. This is proof that you can't generalize about Calcutta. It's a city jerry-rigged never to flourish and never to completely run down.

I open Kalighat's door and step from the freshness of morning into the smell of excrement. Diarrhea, Luke tells me, has been rampant through the night. With the other volunteers I plunge in. I walk a woman to the toilet, then back. Another needs a bed pan *now*. She fills it, and I clean her and empty the bedpan. On it goes. All day the body mantra: wash the women, dress them, wash the mattress, put on clean sheets. Only Salwari is clean—she hasn't eaten for weeks.

Here and then there a woman calls for water. With four other volunteers on their knees I scrub soiled gowns. When noon comes I'm tired, and so are the sick. A volunteer complains of the stink. Luke gives her a look: you came to Calcutta to sniff roses?

Florence Nightingale was born into a family where upper-class women were supposed to play the piano and sing. She perceived her family's privilege as a prison and chose instead a life of engagement. She was right to do so, for kneeling over and over changes the senses' circuits. The one who is whole kneels and attends the one broken, and the broken one attends the one who is whole.

I think of Walt Whitman working as a medic, saying *I become the wounded person.* Becoming vulnerable has a beautiful consequence. It lifts my ego from the fortress of fear and sets it down in Eden's pulsing field. Now the front door opens and a man enters bearing a box. The biscuit factory has sent a donation. I take a biscuit to Hasina. A woman calls out that she needs the latrine, but I don't get there in time. I peel back her soiled gown, wipe her, my hands deep in the grubby details. I and the women feed each other a substance that builds the nerve synapse that blinks the word *yes.*

I keep going down on my knees, and yet I feel like I'm climbing. These women are familiar, and I'm familiar to them. I'm weary, but here where the beds are low and the pace slower, loving is easy. And being loved in return sinks into my skin, flesh, bone.

Luke observes my labor. "Today," she says, "a lot of trouble."

Yes, oh yes, troublesome trouble. Now this trouble has become my bread.

Madurai

Temple Beggar

Midsummer night's heat. We left our shoes at the entrance. The halls were laid out in a cross, four entrances for the four directions. Rows of stone pillars marked the way to the central cella. We had entered holy space.

To go barefoot on stone is to be grounded. I'd have said stoned, but my Indian friends might not have got it. We'd come because Chitra, her husband Nimal and his brother Raj wanted me to see the puja. I knew what to expect. The drumming's relentless and everybody gets way down, whooping, the pusaris in trance, shaking uncontrollably, dancing around on stiff legs, upper bodies flopping like dolls, invoking Mother Kali all fingernails and teeth, tearing the universe to bits.

But we'd come too late. Stalls selling incense were closed, and the women who string garlands on the altar were packing up for the night. I didn't mind. I wasn't in Madurai as a tourist. I'd come to visit the Gandhi Museum where, six months earlier, my friend Betsy Moen Mathiot had died of a heart attack. My grief took the shape of avoiding the tourist spots. I'd spent a few ritual mornings just sitting outside the tiny room behind the Museum where Betsy had lived, watching crows in midday heat pick at rinds. Being attentively present seemed appropriate.

Betsy had established a base in Madurai and made forays out into the villages to research female infanticide. One way it's done, she'd told me, is to drop a grain of rice down the baby's windpipe. I remembered her voice, throaty, like Bacall. She was a handsome woman, together, as we say, and busily productive. She'd lived a life of cheerful outrage, loyal to her Quaker vows. She'd helped several villages start clinics, co-ops, women's support groups. At the Museum she'd founded a state women's organization, the Valliammal Society, which published adult and children's books, operated a pre-school for otherwise abled children, and kept support flowing to the villages. She'd had many friends, and when she died, they'd come together to perform her funeral.

When it came time to light the pyre, there arose the question of who would torch the tinder. If you're Hindu, there's a person whose ceremonial job it is to do this. But Betsy was an American Quaker, these hundred-odd people who were her friends were Hindus, Muslims, Jains, Catholics, atheists, and the ritual was spontaneous and outside official channels. Finally Betsy's friend Chitra went off and bought packages of candles. The candles were distributed, and the mourners formed a ring around the pyre. They lit each other's candles around the circle. Then they stepped forward, each with one candle, and set the pyre afire.

Now petite, pert Chitra and her thin husband Nimal and their friend Raj wanted to show me a good time. "Let's go on, just for a look," Chitra said. "We can explain for you some things about the ceremony."

The Kali temple covers four city blocks and towers above the surrounding streets. Four entrances echo the four directions, and each entrance leads into a hallway of stone pillars that extends all the way to the central cella. Kali is the temple's axis mundi, red fingernails and black teeth poised to tear the universe to bits. The ritual removal of our shoes at the entrance signaled: be advised you are entering the sphere of gods, so leave your ego with your sandals.

A few pillars in I saw the young beggar woman. She was probably in her twenties, though she looked already ravaged. It was partly an act, I knew, but not entirely. Her dirty sari was calculated to attract tourists, but it was also her sari. Then I saw the jutt of matted hair, tied off. My mother would have called this a rat's nest, but here it signaled a sort of infernal deity. It's Hindu practice to marry girls as young as seven to the temple god, and to finalize the marriage vows they tie off part of the girl's hair, which she never combs again. The jutt signals that the marriage has been performed.

The woman was a devadasi, which translates pragmatically as temple prostitute. When Betsy first explained this sacred "marriage," I'd imagined it resembled nuns marrying Christ. Indian girls are supposed to marry, and to bargain for a husband a girl's family needs to provide a hefty dowry. But if the girl is chosen to be a devadasi, the family doesn't have to come up with dowry. Instead they get paid from the temple coffers. They're home free. It's like winning the lottery. The girl gets the privilege of wearing a sari at the early age of seven, which little girls long to do, and other girls and their families are envious. Even boys envy the attention. But the girl can forget school, and there's sex, before she wants it, and she picks up whatever's going around. Nor can she run off and start over: she's no longer a virgin. No one will marry her, even if she has been the wife of a god.

This young woman was someone's abandoned daughter, and she held a tiny, thin girl by the hand, possibly her daughter, possibly a street child purchased from a destitute family. The child was so thin I didn't want to look at her. They sat on the stone floor, the woman talking, the little girl listening intently.

I didn't see the man then, though he must have been close by.

Where there are beggars, policy develops. Some Indians set aside a certain portion of cash to give away each day, some gave when they felt moved to, some refused to give on the principle that begging is a self-destructive practice that shouldn't be encouraged. I'd also witnessed what looked like indifference—smartly dressed, middle-class Indians stepping around a beggar as though that hump of flesh were simply another pile of muddy clay thrown up where the underground drainage system had ruptured. I didn't have a policy. On some occasions I'd rushed past a beggar in the hope that I wouldn't have to confront, just then, the question of my charity. Occasionally, feeling generous and effusive, I'd give away all the money I had with me.

The fact was the little girl was too thin. I had to acknowledge this, and to acknowledge that it was a fact about which I could do little that would permanently improve their circumstances. Still I had a thousand rupee note, about twenty dollars. This argued for dropping a few coins into the woman's hand, then going on to the central cella. Chitra, Nimal and Raj ignored the woman, chatting away as though we were the only ones present.

If I hadn't been there would they have given her something? If I broke away to give her something, would I embarrass them? What, I wondered, would Betsy have done?

The removal of shoes casts us into the commonality. Barefoot on stone, I felt my human nakedness. I was not separate from this space, from the air in the passageway, from the feet of thousands of others who had also walked barefoot on this stone. The repetition of pillars, one after another, began to feel incantatory. This was ritual space, and we were part of the rite. Leaving the lighted entrance, going toward the innermost cella, I turned inward. That I'd passed by the woman without giving made me uneasy. Betsy, I now felt sure, would not have passed by. Betsy engaged what confronted her. Woman by woman, man by man, she had spoken. *We cannot refuse parts of creation and reject other parts. Women and girls are of the creation. The rice grain down the windpipe is a refusal of creation. What gods there are do not want this.*

I was being way too casual about someone else's suffering, and I was not pleased with my self-image. Chitra and Nimal walked ahead, and their portly friend Raj began to explicate the passage from the Gita in which Arjuna is about to go into battle, but hesitates. Arjuna's beloved teacher is on the other side, and Arjuna doesn't want to kill his teacher accidentally. But the god Krishna bypasses this, and says *go and join the battle. Because either you'll die and go to heaven, or you'll live. Either way you'll be victorious.*

"Krishna reminds me of a general beating his breast," I said. "His speech reads like propaganda to convince young men it's heroic to offer themselves as cannon fodder."

Raj's tactic was simply to repeat. "Krishna says if you die, you shall be in heaven. And if you live, you shall be here on the earth in your victorious body."

"Either way you can't lose—I get that," I said. "But Arjuna doesn't want blood on his hands, and I understand that."

"The key," Raj said, "is to become detached. *Detach yourself from the fruit of your actions.*"

Detachment isn't a Western virtue. We think we should attach—attach and take responsibility for our actions. But when we act, we want to make a difference. Betsy was a rescuer. She'd made a difference. I had just declined to make even a teeny difference in the lives of that woman and her child.

Though I'd begun to suspect that in India, if you do make a difference, it will be a difference the size of a pea. Even if you're in a position to endow a school, this sum instantly disappears into the vast suffering that surrounds you as you walk a little way off the main drag in any Indian city. At best this fact can invoke humility: you're reduced to dropping a few *pais* into the palm of the nearest one-legged man. The smallness of that gesture reminds you how insignificant you are.

But this was the application of logic. Betsy would not have bowed to logic. She would have gone forward on her personally devised sacred logic which encouraged helping miracles along. How could I presume to know what would or would not be significant for the woman and her child? I couldn't. And therefore I ought to have simply acted generously and given her something. Charity is the kind of thing you shouldn't think about, I reminded myself. Just do it.

The drumming at the central cella, Chitra had warned, would be relentless, and I'd expected those priests called *pusaris* in trance, whooping, shaking and flopping like dolls. But when we arrived at the holy of holies where they burn the camphor and smear their foreheads with ash, the *puja* was over, the crowd dwindling. Chitra, Nimal and Raj filled me in with anecdotes about the various figures, and I dutifully studied the mannequins' painted nails, a god's four blue arms, Mother Kali's teeth, but I couldn't get interested.

The three of us started back past monolithic pillars, colonnade after colonnade. Was the woman the child's mother? The man might have bought the child from a family desperate for money. It happens. Ahead I saw the entrance. Where scarcity prevails, scams are inevitable, and this one was as stylized as Kabuki. The little girl was curled on the stone floor, asleep. The woman's arm lay across her back as though to protect her. If her gesture was calculated, it was a brilliant touch. But maybe it *was* real. There was no way to know.

The body is transitory and insubstantial, but while you are in it, it feels real. I was glad that woman over there wasn't me. Then

I looked at the woman and thought *that could be my body*. Actually, I thought, that *is* my body.

Then I saw the man a little way off, disappearing behind a pillar. He was giving me room. I despised how he'd planned it, but I couldn't change that, and I couldn't leave it either. I had a thousand rupee note, about twenty dollars. It wouldn't do much, though it would do a little something. But I also had to acknowledge that the money wouldn't be hers for long. Ultimately it would belong to the man.

Possibly the woman had made her quota and I constituted an overage. Possibly she was torn to pieces by the hunger in the child's eyes and her own failure to provide. Possibly she believed in the inevitability of karma and so did not experience guilt, but saw her situation and the child's simply as terrain to be negotiated. And possibly she was simply too weary to have scruples and wanted only to sleep, but knew that if she let me pass the man would be angry.

I knew I couldn't have the impossible, but that didn't stop me from wanting it. I wanted this woman to get leverage. I wanted my money to give her an edge on leaving the temple for good and taking the little girl with her. I couldn't have that, but still I wanted her to have the money, just have it. If she were allowed to keep it, that would constitute a modest but tangible victory. It was what Betsy would have wanted, I thought. Betsy would have given her the thousand rupee note and phone numbers and an invitation printed in three languages to come to the weekly women's group meeting.

The man, wherever he'd gone, was probably so good at this that he'd already guessed almost exactly how much money I'd be likely to give her. Suddenly I didn't care. I was undulant. *Krishna, I'm here in my victorious body. And this one's for Arjuna—and for Betsy.*

The woman saw me and stood up. I went to her and pressed the bill into her palm. We stood inside that ancient, Adamite moment. I thought how fleeting human beings are, how none of us will long survive the gods' downsizing. Then I hurled myself after my friends.

The man was probably so good at this that he'd already guessed almost exactly how much money I'd give her. But I hoped he hadn't seen me. If he hadn't, he might not bother to search her. Though he probably would, it was probably what he did, maybe even the part he liked best. He might grope even the child's dress, feel every fold of the woman's sari, each crevice of her body, and he would find the note, unfold it, claim it as his. Even if he were also kind, if he were tender, sometimes, toward the woman, affectionate with the girl, still there would be that other moment I wished to prevent. The moment when he would take the money from her.

We Are So Vast

Forget the billions.
There is only the one.

Bombay it was called then: midsummer's heat, multitudes filling the streets, bustling, jostling. The roundabout jammed with Toyota sedans, antique delivery trucks, bicycles, motorbikes. A stooped, barefoot man pushed a wooden cart piled with mangoes and tomatoes, and I climbed into a three-wheeler taxi—all of us maneuvering around a heifer, wandering through, chewing leaves of jasmine.

Traffic was a twenty-four-hour hell realm, and I bounced and swayed with the taxi's bumping. I imagined Sister Ignatius' hilltop hospice for cancer patients would be a haven of quiet. I'd come from volunteering at Mother Teresa's hospice in Calcutta, where the atmosphere of agape had nudged me into my own generosity, and now I was heading back to the U.S.A. Since you must spend your last night in Bombay, Mother Teresa said, stay at Sister Ignatius' hospice. On that high hill you will find quiet and tranquility.

The driver maneuvered past men in white *dhotis* unloading melons. Here at sea level was the India of Bahrat peasants working their bit of land, the India of the landless without a bed to sleep in, the India of bent, old women hauling bundles of firewood on their backs, and at night lying down beside the road to sleep in ancient dust. I'd come, I'd seen, I'd cared for destitute women, and now I was ready for Sister Ignatius' high, tranquil hill.

We ascended through a wealthy enclave's canopy of Neems and Palms, and the driver pulled up in front of a palatial edifice. He acknowledged my payment with a head waggle and sped away. Then down the front steps came plump Sister Ignatius in a white habit and nurse's cap buoyant with energy.

"Welcome, my dear!" she said with a flourish. "My Bengali father married a woman from Heidelberg, and I am the result!"

"And you're running the Waldorf-Astoria Cancer Hospice?" I teased.

"Yes I am!" she said, laughing. She slung an arm around my waist. "Come. I'll show you the ward. It's a bit more grand than Mother Teresa's."

On Ignatius' estate there would be no climbing three stories to hang laundry on the roof. Her hospice had an elevator that rose grandly to the third floor. Those barefoot women bent beneath loads of firewood would die at sea level, but privileged Indians would die on this high escarpment, cosseted by their customary comforts, which would surely include a morphine cocktail. There had been no morphine at Mother Teresa's hospice, and I did not approve of this. But here, surely morphine would be generously passed around like an after-dinner mint.

Ignatius swung open the ward's carved, wooden door. The ceiling resembled a cathedral's nave and stained glass light poured down on us.

"We lack only Michelangelo's Sistine chapel," Ignatius said. "There God reaches out to Adam." She smiled mischievously. "Or does Adam reach out to God!?"

The dying would die watching the green-brown sway of ocean rolling in, then sliding out. Ignatius pointed to a light-skinned Bengali.

"A physics professor," she said. "He is lonely. Speak to him. He won't live long."

When I bent down, his eyes that drank the sea met mine. We were strangers, one hale, one ill, but though I stood and he lay prone, we were both living, both dying.

"Ocean," I said, "is the one thing in nature that's always moving."

"I am lucky," he said. "I'll die watching and listening to its beautiful grumbling."

The British bequeathed Indians the habit of four o'clock high tea. Ignatius piled a bowl with tangerines, and we climbed to the top floor and entered a room lined on all sides with open windows. Below spread green-brown ocean. Wind ruffled the curtains, and while we drank tea with milk and sugar, I peeled a tangerine and gave Ignatius some.

Through the weave of her goodwill ran a wide, red band of upbeat outrage. To her mind God was not doing enough to forward Operation Life, and was investing more than she liked in Operation Death.

"So you don't like death?" I teased. "You're in the wrong business."

Her eyes twinkled. "I will tell you my opinion of abortion. It happens to some in some places and not to others in other places, and either way I bow to God. The world is not consistent, far from it. So at any given place and time I accept how things are."

"This is blasphemy!" I teased.

"So much the better!" Ignatius teased back. Then she turned serious. "I am not a true Catholic. I criticize God. The suffering of bodies dying I can bear. But I'm against death by wars. More children die in wars than soldiers."

"God seems to like armies," I said. "Armies are his videogame."

She laughed. "Oh you are wicked!"

"And it's war that keeps some people poor and hungry."

She nodded. "And war is killing rivers and trees and creatures."

"Whales," I said, "and coral beds. We are killing even the air."

We went on naming our lost ones and listing our preferences. We were partial to Flame trees, outraged at the decimation of sea cows.

"I would have made a good Catholic," I said. "I go into cathedrals and temples to feel the atmosphere of worship. I like to genuflect, to do the Hindu's deep bow. I acknowledge the spiritual realm's intangibility. I don't need certainty."

We leaned on the windowsill and watched the brown, light-slung sea. Like a huge lung it breathed in fits and starts. Now a gust of wind blew the curtains inward. Ignatius pointed. Far out on the ocean stood a towering pillar of monsoon rain. We watched this gray mass advance. As it came closer it loomed larger, and as it came closer still, we heard the whirr of water rushing through the air.

Then it was upon us: downpour, loud and huge, banged the roof. Wet sound pounded the Flame trees, the Palms, the ground. Though the eave was wide, we got wet, and we laughed and stayed at the window, drunk with the resolve that is a kind of love.

When the mass of water headed into the city, its sound slowly diminished. We listened to water drip from the Flame trees' leaves, from the tips of Palm fronds.

"We must live big, you and I," I said, "big in every direction."

"Yes," she said, "and wherever we are, we'll kiss the broken bodies. We'll love the broken things of this world."

At dinner I told Ignatius that Mother Teresa ran her hospice entirely on donations.

"Mother says that God will provide. But God didn't donate morphine."

"To die without pain is easier," Ignatius said. "But what we most need is love."

"Surely along with love everyone deserves morphine!" I sputtered.

Ignatius grinned. "God has sent me a spit-fire!" she said. "You want no pain anywhere ever, not at the top of Mt. Everest, nor at the bottom of the deepest sea!"

She had me pegged. I was a Pollyanna insisting that everyone deserved to be pain free all of the time.

"Remember this," Ignatius said. "The only world we have is the one here in front of us right now. Whoever stands before us right now, that one is the Christ nailed to the cross, blood oozing from his side."

I woke into my last day in India, and looked up. Through a jagged crack in the ceiling light poured in. Brokenness was a good thing, I decided, because it let more light into the room. Joyfully I went about showering and dressing in that light. At breakfast I asked Ignatius about her namesake, a soldier who'd quit the army and spent months in a cave, meditating.

"He watched watery air take the form of a cloud," she said, "and in this cloud floated luminous jewels. Buddha tells us that each jewel is connected to all others. Indra's Net, Buddha called it. It tells us there is no way to be alone." She paused. "Please will you say goodbye to the Bengali man?"

It felt as though the Bengali man was the one before me right now.

"Before you go," he said, "will you be kind enough to sing Amazing Grace?"

I was flummoxed. "In India people know this song?"

"In India we like this song very much. I keep the words here on the nightstand."

I lacked a presentable singing voice, and I had never ever sung a solo before an audience. Now a dying man had asked me to sing. Below us, at the bottom of the hill, the roundabout would be dense with trucks, bikes, three-wheeler taxis, wooden carts and the women with bundles of firewood strapped to their backs.

I thought of the heifer in the roundabout, calmly chewing jasmine.

Then I looked up at the ward's high ceiling floating stained glass light.

It's just a ceiling, I told myself. And singing is just singing.

"Amazing grace, how sweet the sound," I sang, "that saved a wretch like me."

There was only a calm sea of silent listeners and my voice. I kept singing. Like everyone else, I was listening to the song's words and my voice filling spacious air with vibrating sound.

"*When we've been here ten thousand years, bright shining as the sun. . . .*"

My voice in those moments seemed an instrument of love, and in the spirit of love, I kept singing. Both of us had found the one we needed most, the one before us right now.

Two Motion Fast Happening God

Calcutta. Sound of the evening gong at the Kali temple next door to the hospice, waves of sound rippling through the roar of bus motors, taxi horns. I was about to head to the bus stand when two aides carried in a woman whose eyes were swollen shut. She couldn't speak. Her sound was a moan.

I offered her water, and she drank eagerly. I brought rice and vegetables and offered a spoonful. She refused it. I tried giving her the plate. She pushed it away. I gave her Tylenol, and she swallowed it with water. Then I led her to the bath, undressed her, bathed her, talking softly. She didn't know my language, but I hoped the sound of my voice would reassure her. I toweled and dressed her in a gown, led her to her cot. I didn't feel I could leave her. I needed a way to comfort us both. I sat on the cot, pulled her to me and began to rock her. Together we found the fulcrum of that rocking, and there, in that two-person motion, we swayed.

Rocking became our language. I had no sense of time passing. Instead time seemed to fill, a reservoir. We swung back and forth, and then came a moment when something shifted: it felt as though she was rocking me. I lay down in that rocking. And after a time I couldn't tell who was rocking whom.

Depending from what viewpoint you might have looked at us, we were either macrocosm, microcosm, or both. We rocked in a sea already rocking, while inside us smaller seas rocked in rhythm with the larger rhythms. In a poem by Rilke, God speaks to creation: *embody me.* In those moments we became the rocking itself. In those moments we embodied the god.

Two motion fast happening god. What god is this? In Kabbalah this back and forth motion is referred to as *ayin*, the nothing that creates the world. *Briah yesh me-ayin*: something continuously created from nothing. This is a special kind of nothing, a nothing that is churning energy. The Yin Yang too is a symbol of these dyadic, churning forces. Buddhist texts describe *annica*: impermanence. Two motions continuously churning the world into impermanent being. Joshu Sasaki Roshi at Mt. Baldy Zen Center in California calls these two forces life and death, or day and night, or mother god and father god. When he speaks less metaphorically, he calls them expansion and contraction.

Sleep is a contractive state, which, as the sleeper wakes, expands. These contracting, expanding energies are around us and in us, and they appear in poems as contractive repetition and expansive variation. Words, these bits of sounding breath, originate and rise from contracted earth, expanding up through this instrument, my body, up through my singing throat, out past my articulating tongue, expanding outward and upward, rising into sky.

The live world embodies this two motion god. I notice when I'm not efficient, when I don't need to know things. When I'm paying attention but not doing anything else. I notice, because I've made myself available. Being available feels like a friendly giving-up of my desires and aversions. My fidgets and small concerns are not important now. I am present in humility, aware that in the great scheme of things I'm minuscule—and also crucial. Sri Nisargadatta articulated this paradox. *Love tells me I am everything, wisdom tells me I am nothing, and between the two my life flows.*

We need moral principles, and whether or not we live up to them, it's important to take responsibility for our actions. But at any given moment I must acknowledge that things are how they are at this moment, that it would make no sense to want things at this moment to be different. I give up my fierce, driven desire to control experience. I give up the illusion that I can prescribe how I'd like experience to be. We can destroy things, but we can't control them. I try to accept this. And in this state of acceptance of the present as it is, I then pay attention to *how* it is.

I perceive that things are fluid and in motion. Beyond the

window I hear leaves breathing, wind dinging the chime. A shaft of light, in motion, reaches across the floor. All this moving everywhere, this exhaling, inhaling: we breathe, the world and I. The world breath comes into me, fueling me with language, and I send this breath out again in the form of a prayer.

If I pay attention to my body, I detect these two motions at different scales: as grand, slow waves, and as tiny vibrations that feel like bubbles continuously bursting. I feel vibrant, alive, present, connected to what surrounds me. And my surroundings, even a littered alley, the pavement gritty—seem beautiful.

Perhaps it's because I'm responsible for my actions that I imagine I do things. But that I imagine I act alone is an illusion. We are not separate agents, but energies in a web of connection. When we think we're giving something away, something is also offered to us. When I put my hands in water, the water washes me. The ground walks me. In sleep I don't have to remember to breathe. The beauty of a crow's arc in the air enters me, sustenance for the soul, and moves a shadowy part of me into light.

When I rocked the woman, I was also rocked. Reciprocity opens me, and in the midst of the world's generosity I feel generous. I perceive that there is great abundance, the result of this sea of offering and receiving. Rocking with the woman felt effortless and very full. I had the sense that the room and everything in the room, including ourselves, had been inflated, and the world seemed infinitely appealing. For our rocking had brought me into awareness of two motion fast happening god.

To be aware at finer and finer levels of discrimination is to approach the paradox of ecstasy. Non-duality: neither speed nor slowness, but both at once. Neither wild nature nor civilized me, just this bittersweet autumn day, the streaming energy of the god.

In this collaboration with the universe I very quickly become filthy rich. The word *filthy* at first seems negative, but when I think about that word, I see that it's full of an overflowing sensuality. When we're engaged in reciprocal perception, language too becomes paradoxical. The word *filthy* suggests the rich muck that nurtures sumptuous gardens. Two motion fast happening god likes this word, a word, which, as I pay attention to it, begins to mean its intended opposite. In just a little while this word *filthy* becomes more and more sweetly clean. Pristine.

Where there is non-duality, there is no "economy." No money changes hands. Air is not deadened by efficiency, nor is light calculated as wattage. No one is counting, and you can step into this love at any moment. When you do, your locked heart opens. You become what in systems theory is called a "flow through." You become the flowing, gathering sustenance from the flowing itself. It's as though we're inside a great touching, and we feel hands, billions of hands, reaching toward us, offering tenderness. We can be here and feel this anytime. Try it, right now.

But we can't always be in ecstasy. Ecstatic states come and go, and when they go, I remember it's time to do the laundry, clean the kitchen floor. Of course these things too are potentially ecstatic moments. But there are times when cleaning the floor feels like just cleaning the floor. And if I compare cleaning the floor to ecstasy, my present state may seem lacking. Since I'm down on my hands and knees anyway, I decide to pay attention to this feeling of lack. I let myself feel it—lack, in all its yawning being—and I keep paying attention. And in a little while there I am in the midst of two motion fast happening god. I work slowly, wet rag in my hand, and keep paying attention. After a while the floor is clean, and I'm abundantly full.

There are times when it feels like the great touching isn't here. I try to pay attention to that absence. As I pay attention, I notice that this absence is somehow substantial, tangible. It isn't just that absence reminds me how fine it was when the god was present, though absence does that. But it's something in itself, this absence. Linda Gregg writes in her poem *The Bounty After the Bounty*, "Our failure was thinking Christ / was his presence. / We were blinded by the actual body / of Jesus." Just as giving has its built-in receiving, absence is also presence. When I look at what *seems* god's absence, the more I pay attention, the more this absence begins to resemble abundance. Very soon absence and abundance become identical, and they're in motion: Two motion fast happening god.

The poet Kabir writes this: "There's a moon in my body / but I can't see it: a moon and a sun." He also calls this god of two motions a love swing. "All earth creatures, even the supernovas, sway between these two trees, and it never winds down."

Pain is savage. It grabs us, throws us against the wall. We lie where it throws us down. It declares itself supreme autocrat. It holds us so that we may not look away, and does not respond to pleas to subside.

When pain insists, it is without mercy.

Pain is the most undeniable form of the god.

And in it, as in everything, the swing swings.

And when pain goes, the swing keeps swinging.

Sometimes when I put up a love swing, things shift. The world turns liquid, and I can't tell myself from the rest of things. My "self" doesn't seem to be there. I've become "the I that is we," and we are one continuous rocking. And yet I stand up, drink a glass of water. I note a passing ant, salute a blue jay. It's as though I'm not there, and yet I'm a personality like no other, going about enacting myself.

Sasaki Roshi explains the god as "zero." Zero is the state of things when expansion and contraction come together, touch and for a while neutralize each other's motion. In Buddhism this zero state is called *samadi.* When we're in that state, things happen effortlessly. We've forgotten linear time passing. It's as though we aren't here, and yet we're extremely, serenely present. In Mark Doty's *Nocturne in Black and Gold* he writes: "No one's here, / or hardly anyone, and how strangely / free and fine it is / to be laved and extended, furthered. . . ."

Eventually, though, expansion and contraction part, and where they part two worlds are created: the worlds of space/time. Contraction is the past, and inside. Expansion is the future, and outside. And when these two worlds are created, there is also a third world: the present, and right here. It's when the present and here come into being that we imagine we have a self. But in fact the present and here are all the "self" we have.

I once helped prepare a meal for five hundred people. The cooks in charge gave me and an old man the task of peeling five hundred boiled eggs. We sat facing each other in the shade of a Margosa, the tub of eggs beside us, and between us another tub into which we laid the peeled eggs.

We were two motions facing each other, become the act of peeling eggs. Though someone watching us might have said each of us separately peeled one egg and then another, they would have been wrong. The old man and I were nothing making something. At one point I looked at his hand, peeling the last bit of shell from an egg, and in that moment the time we call "linear" stopped: the egg in his hand opened into that place in which time is eternal. The atmosphere there was very rich, and there was no need to hurry because eternity—all of it—was right there.

Eventually though, lunch had to be served. I came back into linear time, and the old man and I got on with our work. Gradually the Margosa's shade began to give way to sun, and then came a moment when there was one egg left. I watched the old man pick it up and peel it, then lay it on the pile of peeled eggs. The earth had turned enough by then that most of the eggs in the tub now stood in the sunlight.

Romola

Renegade in the People's Republic of China

The Seventies have slid into the Reagan Eighties, my twins have graduated from high school, Riva's eleven, and in spite of John Lennon's death and the fact that ketchup has been declared a vegetable, the world seems a good, lit place. One day a colleague in the English Department hands me a Stephen Dobyns poem, where a single line rises from the page: *Truly how terrible is the tyranny of the pleasant.* That does it—Peter and I are ready to go beyond our small academic selves, to billow, balloon, fly.

In the twenty-first century historians will document the awful extent of Mao's wrath, but in the Sixties when Americans questioned everything, we wondered would China succeed in creating a socialist paradise? We'd read Orville Schell's descriptions of the PRC and Mao's *Little Red Book,* then observed with dismay as Lin Biao and Mao's wife Jiang Quing organized Red Guards to counter Mao's enemies. This Gang of Four seized control of the Communist Party and the government, and in the ensuing violence, economic activity came to a standstill. Red Guards closed the universities and publicly humiliated professors, journalists, writers, intellectuals.

Now China needs to reconstitute its universities, and Peter and I sign on for a six-month stint teaching at Tianjin's Foreign Language Institute. Hilary works at a bank and declines our invitation, but her twin, Kristen, Peter's daughter from his first marriage, and my daughter Riva who's eleven come along.

Give us spreading distance, give us expansion, give us the Beijing airport at midnight on the first day of January 1982. We arrive like products shipped to a warehouse. The terminal is Marxist drab and without heat. Inside my down parka I'm shivering. Riva's eyes have that beady, bright look of a kid about to collapse.

"Can we drink the water?" she asks. "Will there be noodles? Will they have electric blankets? Is there chocolate in China?"

She wants to sleep, but there aren't even any *chairs.* Are there *beds* in China? Kristen brushes her sleek, black hair, certain now that only a fool goes off to the boondocks with *parents.* She should have stayed where the milkshakes are.

A two-hour train ride south from Beijing brings us to Tianjin, China's third largest city, population seven million. This city is monolithic drab—no yellow, orange or blazing fuchsia anywhere, but then it's winter. The Institute's new apartments for Foreign Experts have heat, but the building is full, so they house us in an elegant structure built during the German Concession. We have lots of room, but the radiators don't work and the electric current can't handle space heaters. Classrooms, it seems, aren't heated either. Peter, the most tolerant person I know, is livid.

"I feel I have to produce heat for us," I say, "but how?"

"Don't worry, Mum," Riva says. "We're all in this together."

"We're going to live in our down coats," Kristen says with resigned *elan.* "We'll wear them eighteen hours a day and maybe even sleep in them."

Silently the River of Heaven turns in the Jade Vault, Su Tung Po wrote, but here no one quotes him. Admiring poetry is still associated with the "decadent" scholar-official class. Fiction, though, is acceptable in the Workers' Paradise because it can teach simple moral lessons. Textbooks bristle with examples of heroic self-sacrifice. Nathan Hale, regretting he has but one life to give for his country. And William Tell: "Father! I'm sure you can do it! Shoot at the apple and hit it!"

Our first morning here we go into the pouring of dark blue Mao suits spilling off sidewalks onto pavement and weaving among the thousands of Flying Pigeon bikes. The Mao suits suggest the triumph of compliance over novelty, the communal over the individual. The Mao suits are *de rigueur*: uniformity cancels fashion, and reminds me that the Cultural Revolution was political correctness hell. Children were terrorized into spying on their parents, and families broke apart.

Now China is gearing up to join the rest of the planet. The boulevard moves human cargo, feeding this energy into factories, labs, hospitals, schools. While one shift works, another shift sleeps, and a third is on the way to work or on the way home. The four of us intend a short walk, but a young man accosts us.

"My name is Wong! When are you born!? I am born 1863!"

There's a saying that one Chinese is never out of sight another Chinese. The crowd gathering around us pushes in. We're the first *why gwo ren* they've seen. A woman and a grandfather reach out and feel a handful of Riva's long, blonde hair.

"Mum! Help!"

I embrace Riva and gesture NO vigorously to the touchers. Others also push in, challenging our Western sense of what constitutes proper distance. We forge into a restaurant to get a handle on our overwhelm, and the restaurant guard shuts the door behind us.

"Wow," Kristen says. "I feel sorry for you, Riva. This is the first time in my life I'm glad I'm not a blonde."

We are *why gwo ren,* curiosities. The right to privacy so prized in the West doesn't exist here. Life in China is lived communally, and privacy isn't on the menu. The girls and I are learning to squat with Chinese women and pee communally. And if I go out the gate, thinking I'll take a short walk, a perky female student takes my hand.

"You must not go alone," she says. "Here we do everything together."

There is no unemployment insurance here because the state gives every Chinese an "iron bowl," meaning a job—work for a lifetime. China is also the nation of the thermos. I imagine those Chinese across this great nation in charge of boiling drinking water: how many are they and what are they paid? We drink the boiled water, mesh with the coal smoke, and every morning Riva pockets her Rubik's Cube and goes off to Chinese school with Chris from Philadelphia and David from Honolulu.

Peter, Kristen and I head out to teach in our down coats. The Chinese teachers of English in my Teachers' Training class range from age twenty to fifty-nine. Before China broke with the Soviets, all foreign language teachers taught Russian. After the break the government ordered all teachers of Russian to begin teaching English immediately. Most of them managed by listening to BBC radio's daily lessons. They'd get a lesson under their belts, and next day teach it verbatim, including the Brit accent.

China's schools were closed for seventeen years, and the Cultural Revolution forced Chinese to toe a strict line. I get a taste of their learned political correctness in my undergraduate English class. These students like it that grammar operates by strict rules. Getting it right feels crucial to them, and lingering fear from living through the Cultural Revolution makes them anxious. We focused on the use of *each* and *every*.

"_____ comrade must prepare a report," a student recited. "Which is it?"

"Either one," I said. "Each comrade must. Every comrade must."

"Before we started across the grassland," a student recites, "each soldier had a small bag of rice. Is that right?"

"Yes," I say, "but the word *every* is also right. Either one will do." Though I'm that sterling being, a native speaker, they want only one answer, the right answer. I try for compromise. "If you really want to be emphatic," I suggest, "use both. Each and every comrade must prepare a report. Before we started across the grassland, each and every soldier had a small bag of rice."

They look dubious. But Liu Xia-Rong gets excited. "I like! We can do both!"

Liu studies a sentence from *Huckleberry Finn.* "'Huck, hidden behind the rock, listened.' Why isn't it *hiding* instead of *hidden*? Shouldn't we use present participle?"

The others are shocked: she dares question Mark Twain!? The Grammar Politburo swings into action.

"No, comrade," Wu says, "it's *Huck hidden* because the main verb is in the past tense. *Huck listened, hidden. . .*" Wu reminds me of my father. He's on point now, and he's going to stay there and see this through.

"But it's not adverbial," Liu says. "Here it's not modifying the verb."

"I disagree with you, Comrade Liu. He's already *in place* when the sentence begins. He's been hiding for some time already."

American students do not debate grammar with passionate intensity. How I like these Chinese students' investment, their fierceness.

Liu persists. "But the grammar book says adverbials always—"

"Surely you know this!" another student says. "*Huck hidden*! We've studied this profusely!"

"Yes, Comrade," Liu says. "But in *this* one case—"

"Comrade! *Huck hidden*! This is the correct way!"

"Still, in this *particular* adverbial—"

"Comrade!" Wu says. "We've been over this! Remember, this book is a masterpiece! Mark Twain, Comrade! Mark Twain doesn't make mistakes!"

I'd expected to meet Zhou En-lai, Lu Xun, the Empress Dowager. Instead the Brit accent Chinese picked up means that I greet the Oriental Winston Churchill, the Bertrand Russell of the Far East, the Sino Queen Mother. Petite, bright, fifty-nine-year-old Shui Shi Ta engages me after class. Feistiness isn't much visible among female Chinese, and the Cultural Revolution cowed most men, but she burns spunk like it's oil. Her permanent wave signals admiration of the decadent West, and she's taken the name Romola after the heroine in George Eliot's novel. But the name has cost her.

"People will want to tell you about their persecution," she says, "because we are still afraid to tell each other. In the Cultural Revolution we learned not to trust."

"The one you thought was a friend could be the one who would turn you in?"

"Yes. In my own case, when I was a student, I admired Mao. He wanted China to become a model society in which all Chinese were equal and the country's wealth shared equally. Of course I wanted to join the Party. But my parents had immigrated to France, and my two sisters married Westerners. This was heresy. You were not supposed to admire capitalism. As a consequence of my sisters' marriages, I was forbidden to join the Party. I should have understood then that Mao was less than perfect. And the Party apparatus controlled who might join. Anyone with Western leanings was suspect.

"When China and Russia were allies, I taught Russian, but I'd also learned English from the BBC and from books on my own. In secret I worshipped Shakespeare."

"And George Eliot," I say, laughing. I'm aware that many Chinese are still wary of socializing with decadent Westerners, but Romola isn't one of them. After class I invite her to visit our apartment soon, and she accepts.

When Riva was five she saw the Thanksgiving duck turning on its spit, and slumped. I don't want to eat animals any more, she said. We'd imagined China a vegetarian's heaven, but the staple is pork. At a restaurant I'd begged a waiter to cook a vegetable dish for my vegetarian child, but he declared that vegetables are always cooked with meat. This *why gwo ren* wracked up forty years on the planet and doesn't know this?

In the freezing temperatures here Riva and I need fat, so I sign on to eat Szechwan pork every day. But Riva sticks to her vow. She lives on noodles, scrambled eggs, milk and *ping gwo li*—fruit that's a cross between a pear and an apple.

This is hard on my string bean child, and she has only one Chinese girlfriend, Wang Rong. Every child wears the red scarf that denotes the Party's Young Pioneers, and Wang Rong has three red stripes on her sleeve: top of the line. Riva affectionately refers to her as Goodie Goodie. She visits us at the Institute—which probably requires permission. After all, we're from America where decadence reigns, as in this student composition:

> In America a woman is liberated. A woman doesn't have to do work in the house because of labor-saving machines. If her husband beats her badly she divorces him and goes to another city. She goes to University to study the science of physics and micro-computer. She is free to join the movies if this is her wish. Later she buys a washing machine, electric blender, bread toaster and cocktail shaker. In her kitchen there is an appliance island. She buys many clothes and expensive. She can own everything and go to California to get suntanned.

When Romola comes, we sit in our freezing apartment with our coats on, and I show her the essay.

"We have been taught that the West is decadent," she says, "so naturally students focus on Westerners' indulgence of their wealth. The Red Guards drilled this into us. They came at me through my nine-year-old daughter. They questioned her about my love of Western literature. She was afraid her friends would shun her because her family wasn't correct. So she turned me in. It felt as though my daughter threw me away.

"But I can't blame her. The Guards scared her. They believed they were carrying out Mao's socialist mandate, and did not admit to themselves that they also threatened and humiliated us because power thrilled them. And they were under pressure from the leadership. Some of them worried about what they were doing, but they had to go ahead."

Like many intellectuals, Romola was exiled to the countryside. Artists, scholars and teachers did peasants' work, ate peasants' food. You no longer had an iron bowl. You were a prisoner doing forced labor.

"They locked me in a bare room for sixteen months and ordered me to read Mao's works. Every day they tested me. But I already knew his writing, and I could quote everything from the Little Red Book. I argued that Mao's good ideas were being betrayed. The guards didn't like that. They made me keep reading, and that challenge made me stronger. Because I was truly an admirer of Mao."

"How did you manage those long months?"

"I cleaned my cell and did exercises. And I sang. I know arias from Chinese operas and from Mozart, and I sang them in my locked room to keep my spirit strong. I also recited Shakespeare I'd memorized. I exercised the muscle of my heart."

"Finally," Romola says, "they let me out and sent me to the doctors to learn medicine. I saw how hard the peasants' lives were. Eighty percent of the population is peasant, and their lives improved under Mao. But now the Party is corrupt. The powerful live like kings and neglect the peasants."

I hadn't understood that first day of class just how daring her lust for English was in a culture which has excised the spiritual realm. Mao and his cohorts were Marxists, and religion was the opiate of the people. The country's temples are still closed.

"I'll have to keep my Buddhist meditation secret here," I say.

Romola smiles. "It's not allowed. But some Chinese still worship in private."

"And your daughter? Are you close to her now?"

Romola shakes her head. "It was hard for her to be a child of a humiliated parent. I have forgiven her, but she cannot yet forgive me."

"Have you noticed," Riva says, "that all Chinese men smoke?"

She and Chris and David come from school, do their American homework, then hang out. Today she confesses that the decadent Triumvirate sneaked into the Institute's supply room, and, in the spirit of "making a statement," she sat on a carton of cigarettes and smashed it.

The Institute head pays a visit and informs us that the kids' prank "must not happen again."

"She just wants to save two billion Chinese men from slow death by lung cancer," Peter says.

Chinese medicine's bottom line is rest. The first time I got sick and missed class, slender Romola and chubby Kwei-Chen arrived with a bag of apples the class bought for me. They were shocked that I was sitting up in a chair, reading.

"You must have a good rest!" Romola said, pulling at my sleeve.

"You must lie down!" Kwei-Chen shrieked, her bangs cut straight across forehead emphatic as her voice.

"I think I will," I said. I was losing my voice. Wonderful, I thought, rescue away!

"Shui, get her some hot water, quick," Kwei-Chen said. "You mustn't drink tea or coffee or chocolate, just hot water."

"You mustn't grade any papers," Romola said.

"Don't talk," Kwei-Chen said. "Rest, and take lots of Yin Qiao for your cold."

"Tonight, Romola said, "I'll bring medicine for your voice."

They were hundreds of bells pealing at once. I basked in their affection and took my Yin Qiao. Japanese import it by the pound. Also Peng Dai Hao, tea for the voice. Teachers, singers and politicians swear by it. Veytalo for ulcers, Huang Lien for vertigo and tinnitus, swollen gums, ulcers of the mouth, acute ophthalmia, constipation, reddish urine. And there's Essence of Chicken to restore youthful vigor to the face.

The back door is a friend in the Party, at the grocery, the pharmacy. Through the back door you get sides of beef, tickets to championship volleyball games, an apartment, and herbal medicines. Romola returned at sunset with a small white bag of Peng Dai Hao and other mysterious packages. She filled one drawer of my desk with vials, teas, tiny cylindrical cardboard boxes of herbal pastes, bags of powders.

"Where did you get all this?" I whispered.

"Oh," she said, mysterious and proud. "I had to go back door."

The second time I came down with a cold, Kwei-Chen and Romola went back door again and returned with bags of herbs to be boiled in a medicine pot.

"Very busy today at the hospital," Romola said. "A lot of people have colds. Lines of people waiting in the halls. People have to wait in line two or three hours."

"But when we told Xiao Xin you were sick," Kwei-Chen added, "she went right out and came back with the medicine immediately."

I am such a marvelous foreigner, it seems, that I have become that much coveted corruption, the back door.

"Which one of you is the front door?" I teased, "and which the back?"

They laughed, and then Kwei-Chen laid down the law. "Chinese medicine insists that when you are sick you must rest. Do not come to class for many days until you are well. This is how we do it here. We who are students will use the time to study."

The West's ubiquitous rev is absent here. I'm used to six hours a week in the classroom, not counting prep time and grading, but here it's fourteen hours. Even so, work feels easier and time seems slower. I feel less driven, more open.

Romola comes to our apartment for tea. I tell her I met a man carrying an old woman piggyback. Her teeny feet had been bound.

"Huang O," Romola said. "You know this poet?"

Huang O lived during the sixteenth century's Ming dynasty when bawdy comedies and erotic novels were the rage. But women who weren't courtesans didn't write erotic poetry—except for Huang O. *All night the cock's gorgeous crest stood erect. I will let you undress me and unlock my sealed jewel.* I know only Rexroth's translation.

"Her feet," Romola says, "measured three inches. Peasant families don't do this because women must work, but in the upper classes no one would marry a girl without bound feet. And it was mothers, grandmothers and aunts who had to break the bones and wrap the bandages tighter. I am so glad I didn't have to do this to my daughter."

The snow quits. Dusk is clear, pure cold. The white courtyard beautiful. No Chinese woman wears jewelry, scarves, hair ornaments now—that would reek of decadence. But today Romola defies this prohibition.

"Your hairpins are elaborate," I say. "So beautiful and so unusual here."

"Even Mao said jewelry was decadent. But these are special Phoenix hairpins, from my grandmother. Now I wear them for you."

It's the coldest day of the year and my birthday. Riva comes from school and we eat chocolate and split an orange soda.

"I hate this cold," she says. "But it's nice that I have you to myself sometimes." She pulls out her American homework and shows me a sentence she's tried to diagram. *Reagan has made a total mess of the economy!* "Mum, I'm wasting time at Chinese school. Can I stay home some days and do my American homework instead? I don't want to fall behind."

I say yes. It's as though amidst slabs of pork I manage to find her favorite food, an artichoke. She bursts into improvisational dance, then goes to look for Chris and David. That evening Romola arrives bearing a large box. She opens it with a flourish. Chinese do not eat cake, but Romola has strong-armed a baker. She displays this weighty cake, built, it suggests, by a construction company of bakers, substantial enough to feed a platoon of Red Army soldiers. The five of us dig in, our mesh flowery with chat and laughter. Romola tells us that her husband also admired Chinese opera, and applauded her recitations of Shakespeare. But he died before the Cultural Revolution.

"What kind of work does your daughter do?" Kristen asks.

"She drives a drilling rig."

I imagine this young woman in the rig's cab, steering this powerful piece of machinery, encompassed by its grinding noise. Chances are she's not singing an aria.

"Does she like that work?" Riva asks.

"I don't know," Romola says. "She does not tell me."

This, for the daughter of a woman who today in class recited Hamlet's soliloquy—all of it. She leaves, and I feel the tug of her blue jacket going down the stairs.

"Romola loves you," Riva says. "She wants you to be her Chinese daughter."

The snow's melted, and there are buds on the shrubbery. Off come our down parkas! One morning I walk onto the balcony and look down. The quad has filled with students, but the Mao jackets are gone. Men wear dark cotton pants and short-sleeved white shirts, women flowered skirts and white short-sleeved blouses.

Peter lumbers out in pajamas. "Amazing! Spring comes when the Party says so. They've told a billion people exactly which day to take off the long underwear."

A few weeks later in the Institute's gardens May's heat opens the water lilies. I've barely begun to glimpse the nuances of Han culture, but on the human scale I've weighed in. And the live world's scale—that mesh in which we continuously adjust our sync and linkage—that's the scale that matters. Riva and Wang Rong—Goodie Goodie—get permission to plant beet seeds in front of the office. They dig with trowels and giggle. When they've seeded the row, Riva takes her friend's hand and brings her upstairs for orange soda.

Now that the sun has delivered 80 degrees Fahrenheit, Riva and I are blossoming.

"I just wish for once I could drink a really cold beer," Kristen says.

Chinese believe cold drinks are bad for health. They sip beer at room temperature. Only in upscale hotels can barbarians partake of that delicacy the ice cube. The girls seem eager to go home, but I'm conflicted. I've synced into the mesh of this place, and the earth here has taken me in. In spite of a lingering political correctness, I've become larger, more clear. And in the living, breathing mesh, Romola and I have come together. She's been Mother, Godmother, Guide—diminutive in stature, large and abundant with love and resolve. I came here longing to expand, and I'll leave fed by her example: her voice lifting a cluster of notes, singing them into the air.

The young teacher of German takes up with a Chinese graduate student, and when they announce their plans to marry in Germany, campus buzzes with scandal. For Hans, intermarriage with a Westerner constitutes the advance war party coming to tear down The Great Wall. Hence the question plump and bespectacled Zhu Li-chen poses in class.

"Do black people and white people get married in the U.S.?"

"Yes, they do," I say.

"But they're different," Zhu says. Is it the thick lenses that give him that dazed look? "How can they talk?"

"Of course they can talk, Zhu," Romola says.

I feel a swell of happiness. A class becomes a country, this country belongs to all of us collectively, and intensity forges intimacy. I'm on my knees, hands in the Chinese dirt, my mind mingling with theirs.

"But they're not the same," Zhu says. "So how can they marry?"

No self-respecting Han would marry out. But I decide to push the envelope.

"They're people," I say. "All people are human. Black people and white people fall in love like anyone else. Suppose you were single and you fell in love with a Tibetan or a Mongolian. You'd want to get married."

Thin, inscrutable Wang stands up. "Mongolians want to marry Mongolians, and Hans want to marry Hans."

I think of Martin Luther King's voice invoking our "single garment of destiny." To remind them that Americans too struggle with racism, I offer an example from the Civil Rights Movement: white men who murdered Emmett Till, then grinned and kissed their wives for the cameras.

"Hatred happens in my country too," I say. "But hatred that fierce comes from fear. It's fear that makes us suspicious of each other. Think about it. Why feel afraid of a Mongolian? You're not afraid of me, are you?"

"We like you very much," Kwei-Chen says. "We would like to marry you, but you already have a husband."

The students laugh and the tension dissolves.

"I knew a teacher at my school who became in love with a Laotian," Kwei-Chen says. "The Laotian teacher taught at our school for one year. They married and the woman went with her husband to live in Laos. I think she can be very happy there."

"It's not possible!" Zhu insists.

"The fact that we are having this discussion at all is a sign of your courage," I say. "Now think about all these different people here on your continent. Hans, Mongols, Laotians, Cambodians, and so on. Who did you all come from?"

Zhu looks confused. He knows exactly who *his* ancestors are. He can trace them back seven generations, and they're all Hans. I once asked him how long his family had lived in Tianjin. Five hundred years, he replied.

"Your ancestors, way back. Who were they? Who was your great-great-great-great-great-great-grandfather?"

Romola grinned. "Peking man," she said.

The day we left Tianjin was windy. Unusual, this wind, rearranging the atoms in and around us. I'd taken so much Chinese medicine and eaten so much Szechwan pork and been loved by so many people for so long, that I felt I'd earned my pinpoint in the mesh. But the wind kept blowing, and the sound of each heat-laden gust was the sound of *annica*: impermanence.

Kwei-Chen was sick that day, but Romola came along to the train station.

"Lao Shui," Peter said. It means Honorable One. He'd tried to call her Lao before, but she'd demurred. Today her smile spoke: all right, kind man, if you insist.

The girls picked out seats, pushed their bags onto the rack.

I looked at Romola—she'd gone up the mountain alone. Then she'd fed herself celestial salads of Shakespeare and music, and on this rich diet grew confidently mighty. Two days before leaving, the students had presented Peter and me each with a scroll. The calligrapher's brush inscribed mine with the poem I'd chosen by Li Ching Chao, *The Sorrow of Departure.* A student read the poem in Chinese and I recited it in English.

Which line of the poem do you like most? Romola had asked.

My hair pins are too heavy I'd said.

Romola nodded. So are mine, she'd said. But you make them feel lighter.

The train was ready to go. Back in Boulder amidst our Chinese red poppies I knew I would feel the tug of her love.

"Romola, imagine I'm your daughter, and I've come to tell you I'm sorry and to ask your forgiveness."

She touched my cheek. "You have been my daughter already many months."

There are two forms of friendship, Simone Weil wrote, *meeting and separation. For those who love, separation, although it is painful, is good, because it is love.*

"Romola," I said, "I'm afraid I'll never see you again."

She withdrew from her pocket the Phoenix hairpins and laid them in my hand.

"Please accept these," she said. "They are too heavy for me now."